Take Your Game to the Next Level!

The Intermediate's Guide to
DOG AGILITY

Laurie Leach

The Intermediate's Guide to Dog Agility

Project Team
Editor: Stephanie Fornino
Copy Editor: Joann Woy
Indexer: Lucie Haskins
Cover and Interior Design: Mary Ann Kahn

T.F.H. Publications
President/CEO: Glen S. Axelrod
Executive Vice President: Mark E. Johnson
Publisher: Christopher T. Reggio
Production Manager: Kathy Bontz

TFH Publications, Inc.
One TFH Plaza
Third and Union Avenues
Neptune City, NJ 07753

Copyright © 2010 by TFH Publications, Inc.

Quoted material in Chapter 27 is reproduced with the permission of Diane Peters Mayer, from her book *Conquering Ring Nerves: A Step-by-Step Program for All Dog Sports*.

Printed and bound in China

10 11 12 13 14 15   1 3 5 7 9 8 6 4 2

Library of Congress Cataloging-in-Publication Data
Leach, Laurie.
    The intermediate's guide to dog agility : take your game to the next level / Laurie Leach.
        p. cm.
    Includes index.
    ISBN 978-0-7938-0637-9 (alk. paper)
    1. Dogs--Agility trials. I. Title.
    SF425.4.L433 2010
    798.8--dc22

The Leader In Responsible Animal Care For Over 50 Years!®
wwww.tfh.com

Table of Contents

Introduction

So you picked up this book and started reading—good move! You have come to the right place if you want to continue improving your understanding of agility and agility skills. In *The Beginner's Guide to Dog Agility*, I wrote about my love for agility. Years later, I feel exactly the same way. I wake up happy on the days I get to attend class with my dogs. I am thrilled when students run successfully with their dogs on increasingly difficult courses. Most of all, I love it when my dogs make it clear that there is nothing they would rather do than race through an agility sequence as fast as they can.

In recent years, our understanding of how to train dogs for agility and how to handle them on course with precision has taken a dramatic leap. Leaders in agility have developed new systems for teaching and handling dogs that are revolutionizing the sport. In writing this book, I have been strongly influenced by international agility competitors and teachers Greg Derrett (www.gtagility.com), Susan Garrett (www.clickerdogs.com), and others. Their work is helping agility handlers everywhere to become faster and more consistent. You can do the same.

I have also learned a tremendous amount from my human students. I have had the joy of working with many from the first day they set foot on an agility field to the time they became competent, joyful competitors. They have allowed me to work with a variety of dogs to test the methods I share in this book. Many of the teaching photos in the book highlight these students and their dogs. All are regular folks like you who came out to have fun with their dogs. We worked through many challenges. Each team is a success story.

It is impossible to ignore my other teachers—my dogs. I am currently training my seventh agility dog, a young Border Collie. I continue to compete with two Shelties who believe that agility was invented for them. On occasion, I will highlight my dogs as examples, not because they are unique but because they are just like your dogs.

Part of the attraction of agility is that you can continue to learn from the day you start until the day you retire. Let's get started taking your agility skills to the next level.

Why You Need This Book

By the end of *The Beginner's Guide to Dog Agility*, your dog had been introduced to all of the obstacles, and you were practicing simple sequences consisting of four to six obstacles. You were practicing using your body language and clicker to communicate with your dog. It is recommended that you master the skills in the first book before you try the exercises in this sequel.

It is my goal to lead you gently up the learning curve from novice to intermediate. By the final chapter, you will understand the skills needed to meet intermediate-level challenges and how to teach them to your dog. You will also have had opportunities to practice these skills in both short and long sequences.

How the Book Is Organized

The book is composed of six sections, each focusing on an important aspect of agility. Although you may find it most useful to read through them sequentially, each section also stands alone so that you can focus on the skills most appropriate for you.

 In each chapter, you will find a reference to an earlier skill or topic from *The Beginner's Guide to Dog Agility*. These references will connect the foundation training you did as a beginner with the new, more complex agility skills you will be learning in this book.

Part One: Hooked on Agility

Prior to heading out to the agility field to tackle more challenging sequences, we will take a moment to consider what you can do to care for your canine partner so that he stays healthy and continues to love playing this game. You will also find a readiness test for your dog. These exercises, done successfully, will provide feedback that he is ready to progress to the intermediate level.

Part Two: Intermediate Handling Skills

This section highlights 12 must-know intermediate handling skills. In each chapter, you will find a thorough description of the skill, with supporting maps and photos. Next, you will find a step-by-step guide to learning the skill and practicing it with your dog. At the end of each chapter, you will find a final example of the skill, which you can use for mental practice or can set up to try with your dog.

Part Three: Preparing for Challenging Sequences

This section focuses on the preparation that experienced handlers do prior to running longer sequences. You will learn how to walk a complex sequence and plan in detail how you will handle your dog. Next, you will learn how to identify the toughest parts of a sequence. Last, you will learn a powerful process called backchaining, which will help you prepare your dog to handle new challenges.

Part Four: On Course

In this part, we will turn our attention to sequences that require two or more intermediate skills. Then you will find several complete courses onto which you will put multiple skills into action. You will find these exercises useful as mental or as real practice.

> **Take Note**
> All the instruction presented in this book is important. However, some ideas have a make-it-or-break-it quality. Throughout the book, watch for a summary of those essential ideas under this heading.

Part Five: Solving Common Intermediate-Level Problems

No matter how well we train, we encounter challenges in teaching our dogs. In this section, we will consider how you can address the three most common problems in agility. Then we will discuss a problem-solving approach to address any other issues that might arise.

Part Six: On the Agility Circuit

In this final section, we will focus on the skills that top handlers use at trials to maximize success. You will learn how to memorize courses, use video to improve your skills, keep your nerves from sabotaging your performance, utilize the warm-up jump, and keep accurate records.

Concluding Thoughts

When I consider the process of growing from a novice-level handler to an intermediate handler, I am aware that there are so many skills to master. Agility isn't just about obstacles and sequences. It is about movement and building an entire system of communication that you can use with your dog at a dead run. It is a long, slow process to learn how to play well, and over time, it is easy to forget how much you have learned.

I often think about the progress one of my students has made. During her first year of training, I frequently reminded this student to direct her dog smoothly by drawing a path rather than flapping her hands at the obstacles. I showed her how to change sides with a front cross without blocking her dog's path. She worked hard for many months to master these and a multitude of other skills you will find in the following chapters. There were plenty of times when human and dog ended up standing still on the agility course and staring at each other, trying to figure out what they were supposed to do next. A few weeks ago, another student joined this student's class for the day. The visitor watched her complete several runs and then commented to me that she was the smoothest handler he had ever seen. She and her dog had learned to flow through each course at a lively pace, making the hardest challenges look easy. In writing this book, I hope to help you do the same.

Since I wrote that first book, *The Beginner's Guide to Dog Agility*, the sport of agility has continued to grow around the world. Despite my early warning that agility could change your life, many of you have allowed yourself to develop an intense passion for the sport. There are a couple of reasons that you have been unable to resist falling in love: You love your dog, and he loves agility! My students often tell me that their dogs go crazy with excitement when they turn on the road to the agility field. You may love the unique partnership that you have developed with your dog learning to play the game. You may love the continuous learning that is an inherent part of this complex sport. And last but certainly not least, you may love that burst of adrenalin that your body produces when you are running a course.

To find out how deeply agility has set its hook in you, consider the following questions. Give yourself one point for each question you answer with a yes.

1. The day you go to agility class is your favorite day of the week.
2. If your agility class is canceled, you are seriously disappointed.
3. You read books and articles about agility.
4. You belong to an Internet agility list.
5. You bring family and friends to watch your agility class.
6. You ask for agility equipment for holiday gifts.
7. You would quit your job in a heartbeat to train more.
8. You frequently think about your "next" dog.
9. You would rather get a high-level agility title than a master's degree.
10. You have purchased a new car/RV for agility.
11. You have an exercise program so that you can run faster on the agility course.
12. You promised the next dog to your partner, but now you are training the pup for agility.
13. You train with two or more teachers.
14. You would rather go to an agility trial than on a vacation.
15. You have moved to an agility-friendly property or area.

If you scored 1–2, it's not too late to maintain a healthy balance in your life, but do you want to? If you scored 3–4, face the facts. You are in love with this sport. If you scored 5–15, you are seriously hooked. There is no turning back! I count myself among the ranks of those who cannot imagine life without agility. Just this morning, I was thinking that I would like a new set of tunnel sandbags for my birthday. If you are in the same boat, read on.

In Part I of this book, we will take a look at three topics. First, we will discuss what it means to be an intermediate-level handler in agility. Second, we will review ten human behaviors that will keep your dog loving agility; the importance of keeping our dogs happy while we ask them to run longer sequences and perform more physically challenging exercises can't be underestimated. Last, we will look at a series of readiness tests that you can do with your dog to determine if he is ready to tackle the next level of skills presented in the book. Let's get started.

Part I

Hooked on Agility

1
What Is Intermediate Agility?

Recently, one of my students who had just started competing in agility e-mailed me after a trial. She had walked from the novice ring to watch the intermediates and was struck by the differences she saw. "The dogs at the intermediate level were running courses that were considerably more complex than what Phoebe and I are doing," she wrote. This was very perceptive.

Before we launch into the specific skills that will take your handling to the next level, let's take a look at the changes you can expect at the intermediate level of agility and when you can officially call yourself an intermediate handler. The leap from novice to intermediate handler is the biggest leap you will make in your agility career. Once you are a solid, confident intermediate, you will find the leap to the excellent level to be remarkably easy.

The Difference Between Intermediate and Beginner Agility

At the beginning level of agility, the emphasis is placed on a dog's ability to perform each obstacle safely and completely. Handlers are often allowed to have one or more mistakes on course and still earn a qualifying score toward a novice title. Courses are fairly basic, with obstacles placed a good distance from each other. Emphasis is on simple lines.

Reading Agility Maps
Knowing how to read agility maps is an essential skill. In the figures in this book, standard symbols are used to represent each agility obstacle; dotted lines represent the handler's movement, while solid lines represent the dog's movement. Using the maps in this chapter, quiz yourself on each symbol. If you're not sure what a symbol means, see the agility obstacle key on page 240 in Appendix I for a review.

There are four significant changes between the beginning level of agility and the intermediate level.

Longer Sequences

When we left off in *The Beginner's Guide to Dog Agility*, you were completing sequences of up to six obstacles. As you move toward the intermediate level, you will gradually extend the number of obstacles you do without stopping until you can handle 15 to 20 obstacles.

Harder Challenges

At the intermediate level, the path a dog must travel is made more difficult. This is done by placing obstacles closely together so that the correct obstacle is not immediately obvious to the

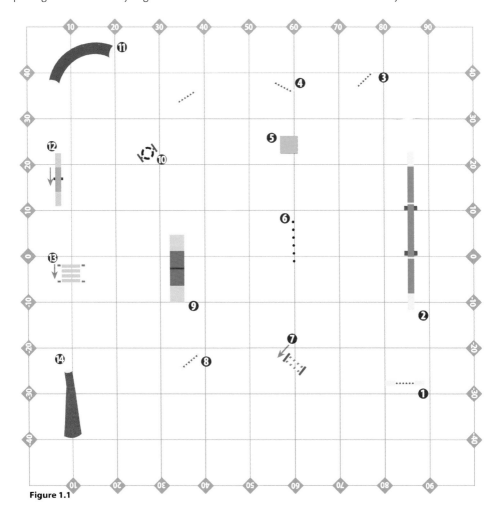

Figure 1.1

Hooked on Agility

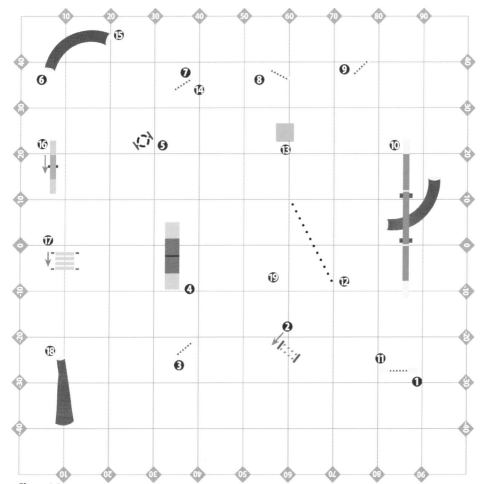

Figure 1.2

dog and by setting the obstacles at more challenging angles. The differences are highlighted in Figure 1.1, a typical novice course, and Figure 1.2, a typical intermediate course.

Maneuvering through the tough spots requires a wider array of handling techniques. In subsequent chapters, you will learn 12 specific handling skills that will allow you to communicate clearly with your dog while you negotiate intermediate challenges.

Fewer Mistakes

Novice-level classes recognize that new teams are bound to make some mistakes. For example, in American Kennel Club (AKC) trials, novice dogs with two refusals may still earn a

In intermediate agility, your partner must perform each obstacle with greater confidence and move quickly between obstacles.

qualifying score. (A refusal occurs when the dog sees an obstacle but hesitates to take it or runs past it.) At the intermediate level, a team is allowed only one refusal.

Faster Times
At the novice level, the time allotted for a dog to complete the course is relatively generous. At the intermediate level, dogs must complete the courses more quickly to qualify. This means that your partner must perform each obstacle with greater confidence and move quickly between obstacles.

Becoming an Intermediate Team
Each of the agility organizations offers competition classes at a minimum of three levels, reflecting beginning, intermediate, and advanced skills. Teams start by competing in each agility game, such as jumpers or the standard class, at the novice level. In each individual game, handlers must complete a novice title before moving up to the intermediate level.

This is where things get tricky. The requirements to complete a title in each game are different in every organization. For example, in Canine Performance Events (CPE), one must earn only two qualifying scores in Level 1 standard to move to Level 2. However, teams need only one qualifying score in jumpers to move up. In AKC competition, teams must earn three qualifying scores in each game to move to the intermediate level. It is typical for a team to be at the intermediate level in one game and at the novice level in another for a period of time.

Once you are at the higher level in a specific game, you compete against other intermediates—sort of. Say that you are an intermediate in United States Dog Agility Association (USDAA) games. Then you decide to start competing in the North American Dog Agility Association (NADAC). Naturally, you must start as a novice. In a real sense, you are an intermediate competing against other novices. Because there is no limit on how many dogs in a class can qualify, this situation often affects only placement ribbons.

What It Really Means to Be an Intermediate

Not everyone chooses to compete in agility. There is nothing wrong with simply playing the agility game with your dog. I have a number of skilled students who don't enjoy competition. If you don't define yourself by your progress through different agility titles, what does it mean to be an intermediate?

There are two questions to ask yourself: Are you and your dog becoming confident running full-length courses with a minimal number of mistakes? Are you and your pup making progress toward successfully handling the type of challenges presented on the intermediate map in Figure 1.2, using the skills presented in this book? If you answer in the affirmative, then you are on your way to becoming an intermediate handler.

Take Note

It is important to note that there are six significant agility organizations—American Kennel Club (AKC), Australian Shepherd Club of America (ASCA), Canine Performance Events (CPE), Dogs on Course in North America (DOCNA), North American Dog Agility Council (NADAC), and United States Dog Agility Association (USDAA)—and several other smaller organizations that sponsor agility trials in the United States. Those are listed in the forms in Appendix II. Several other countries also have multiple organizations that sanction agility trials and present their own set of complexities, and each operates by its own set of rules. As a result, there are many variations in rules. In the discussion in this chapter, most generalities hold true, but always check the specifics before you compete in a new venue.

Concluding Thoughts

The transition from the beginning level of agility to the intermediate level will definitely take your skills to the next level. As you have already learned, teaching your dog the basics of agility is a long, slow, wonderful process. Progressing from the novice level to the intermediate level is a journey that will take many months or even years. Enjoy your partnership with your dog, and celebrate together when you learn a new skill.

2
Caring for Your Agility Partner

As much as I love agility, I love dogs more, and I am sure that you feel the same. In this chapter, we will quickly review the things you can do to keep agility fun for your dog. Remember that you have chosen to participate in the sport of agility—your dog didn't make that choice. He just wants to play with you. If he could, I think he would suggest the following guidelines for you.

Be Fun to Work With

Dogs are body language experts. They are aware of your body language and expressions. They love it when you smile, exclaim happily, laugh, and clap. Find a word that your dog loves, and use it when he runs particularly hard. (I am known for my trademark "Yahoo!" when my pup nails something on the agility course.) Be generous with cookies when he gets something right. Bring out the toys before your dog tires, and play regular games of tug and chase.

If you are an inherently serious person, try to shake this off on the agility course. Frowning, sagging shoulders, or throwing up your arms communicate to your dog that there is a problem. Those behaviors will make him worry, and worry takes the joy out of any game. Work on lightening up when you step onto that agility field.

Don't Blame Your Dog

Mistakes are a human concept. If your dog goes in the tunnel instead of up an A-frame, he thought that you wanted the tunnel, didn't consider the A-frame as much fun as the tunnel, or perceived the A-frame as scary.

Strive to train so that your partner never even knows that something happened that was not what was planned. Try a cheery "Uh oh!" and then race back happily to try the sequence again. You can always do something over and get it "right." But if you take the edge off a dog's initiative and enthusiasm by your reactions, it is very difficult to get them back.

Set your dog up for success by never asking him to do something he is not prepared to do.

Alternate New Challenges With Easy Games

It is tempting to fall into a pattern of training in which the exercises you ask your dog to do get only more difficult. This is mentally exhausting for dogs. Even when your dog gets quite advanced, ideally try to alternate harder exercises with games that allow him to just blast through an easy sequence. For example, you might work several sets of hard entries to the weaves but then let your pup run full speed in a circle of jumps and a tunnel. This will help keep him enthusiastic and enjoying the game.

Keep Your Demands Reasonable

Never ask your dog to do something he is simply not prepared to do. A dog who is pushed too hard may slow down dramatically because he is unsure what to expect, and at worst, may become anxious about certain obstacles. Students sometimes get caught up in a class dynamic and let their dogs get in a situation that is too much too fast. For example, don't put your dog on a teeter that is higher than a level he has completely mastered. Don't ask him to do a sequence of obstacles that is longer than he is able to complete with speed and enthusiasm. I encourage students to tell me if they need to modify an exercise so that their dog can be successful.

Recognize That Dogs Progress at Different Rates

In one of my classes, students were making steady progress, except for a young Miniature Pinscher who had recently been rescued. She just didn't seem to see the point of running through those dark tunnels or even sticking with her handler when there was so much to explore. I could feel her handler's discouragement building. I encouraged her to stick with it, knowing that agility

Hooked on Agility

could be the key to building a relationship with this dog. The handler persisted, rewarding the little girl intensely every time she did one obstacle and then two. Running through a tunnel earned her a cookie party. One day with no warning, the little dog arrived ready to play. She flew through tunnels, nailed her contacts, and raced down lines of jumps. Although she still relapses occasionally, she has definitely turned a corner.

If your pup is slower to develop, stay patient. Remember not to let him see or feel any discouragement because this will make him anxious and less, rather than more, likely to perform. Continue to tell your dog with timely reinforcement that you like it when he plays with you, and he will likely come around.

Emphasize Quality Over Quantity

Not everyone wants or needs a type A agility dog. You can have lots of fun in agility with your easygoing dog as long as you train wisely by stressing quality over quantity and emphasizing fun.

It is essential that you know your dog's stamina limits. If you continue to run him until he is fatigued each time you train, he will start to save himself rather than working at top speed. You will find that you have successfully trained a slow agility dog, which is the opposite of what you want.

If you have a lower-drive dog, choose what to do and what not to do in class so that he stays energetic. This is much harder than it sounds. It is the nature of any group to put subtle pressure on the individuals to participate in every activity. Agility classes are generally an hour or more and often require a dog to repeat obstacles multiple times. The high-drive dog, of course, begs to do the dogwalk 20 times—*Hey, just once more! I know I can get it right.* Other dogs who enjoy agility but do not see it as their full-time work get tired of repetition and slow down rather than speed up. Remember that your dog can't tell you verbally when he has had enough, but his speed and enthusiasm are just as clear a message.

I have a student with a quiet little terrier. I admire her greatly because she consistently makes good choices about how much her lower-drive dog can do. Even when she started competing, she recognized that two days were simply too much for her little girl. By entering just one day, both handler and dog have been highly successful and have earned many titles.

Pay Attention to Your Reward System

Dogs repeat behaviors for which they get paid. Actually, this is true for people too. If you get a check for going to work, the odds are high that you will return. But imagine how motivated

The Clicker
The clicker is a small noisemaker that tells the dog precisely what he did right to earn reinforcement in the form of food or a game. It is more effective than verbal praise because the sound is quicker, and it can mark a specific behavior such as a fast *down* on the table or a blistering run through a tunnel. When a clicker is well used, it leaves little doubt in the dog's mind what behavior you wanted and whether he got it right.

Caring for Your Agility Partner

Reinforcement for your dog can consist of food or interactive play with a favorite toy.

you would be if your boss popped into your office and slapped a check on your desk every time you did something extraordinary. Dogs are just the same. The more your dog understands specifically what behavior you liked because you took the time to "pay" him, the more likely he is to repeat it.

Reinforcement for your dog can consist of food or interactive play. It is ideal if your dog responds to both and you can alternate using them. Remember that something constitutes a reward only if your dog values it.

The challenge is that handlers fall into the trap of trying to finish each exercise before they reward their dog. National level competitor Sharon Freilich writes, "For those that have trained with me, you have probably seen me jump up and down during classes yelling, 'Reward, reward, reward!' The reason is that I saw something brilliant on course that should have been rewarded. The dog might have done a magnificent 270-degree turn, performed an extraordinary serpentine, or perhaps picked up the rear cross cue and performed it well. But what does the handler decide to reward? You guessed it—the last jump. It is important to reward the parts in order to develop the specific behaviors that you want."

It's easy to talk about stopping in the middle of a sequence to reinforce your dog and terribly hard to do. There is something compelling about driving ahead to the end of an exercise. The problem is that dogs who are rewarded only at the end of every exercise get sloppy and disinterested until they approach the final obstacle. The best way to counter this tendency is to make a plan before you run. As you walk the sequence, identify which section you would like your dog to do well or that will be a particular challenge. If he gets it right, use your clicker or marker word to highlight the behavior, whip out your toy and play, or offer a cookie. Then regroup and continue on your way to the end of the exercise.

Continue With the Clicker

Did you catch the previous reference to your clicker? I hope that you are continuing to use it or a consistent marker word as a powerful communication tool as described in *The Beginner's Guide to Dog Agility*. It continues to be the best way to tell your dog how pleased you are with what he has done. Interestingly, I notice that my students tend to lose track of their clickers or marker words after the first few months of class. This is a serious mistake.

Dogs are simply not wired to understand our endless chatter. On the other hand, a dog taught with a clicker or marker word hears the sound as: Bingo! It leaves no doubt in his mind that something good happened. As you continue your agility training, your clicker or marker should be used as you did before to mark a specific behavior and to tell your dog that you will reinforce him for that performance.

Remember That Retraining Is Part of the Game

In training classes, students often say, "I know he knows that" after their dog does something unexpected. They have forgotten a key fact: Learning comes and goes.

Dogs and people learn, forget, learn, forget, and finally learn something so that it becomes internalized. Learning is rarely a linear process.

Understanding this will save lots of frustration. Your dog is likely to weave nicely one day and look completely baffled the next day. This past weekend, my younger Sheltie, who has never missed a weave pole entry in a trial, suddenly saw no difference between entering between the first and second poles or second and third poles. Oops.

Once your dog shows you that he has forgotten something, don't just keep trying. Simply loop back to your previous training and help him get it right. Reinforce generously with cookies. When the lightbulb goes back on, you can offer a bigger challenge.

Build Proofing Into Your Training

Proofing is the process of teaching your dog to behave as you have taught him even if there are many tempting distractions nearby. As you know, this is very important in agility because trials are highly stimulating places. Dogs must know how to run a course with a flying disc game nearby, a dog running in the next ring, or a crowd cheering.

Handlers often think that their dog knows a command until he is asked to do it in a new location or with lots of distractions. It rarely goes well when handlers try to leap from taking a class to participating in a trial.

As your pup learns new intermediate skills in agility, give him as many opportunities as possible to practice in different settings. These may include taking lessons from a second teacher, enrolling in seminars, and even hauling small equipment to the park to practice.

Concluding Thoughts

It is not always easy to remember all this advice. I had a personal experience with this just this year. I finally got a Border Collie after years of yearning for one, and I found myself wanting her to be perfect right off the bat. I got serious and started to push harder than her puppy brain could handle. Fortunately, I came to my senses and saw that she was not enjoying our training sessions. As soon as I returned to having fun and became reasonable in my expectations, she became a learning sponge.

This experience reminded me of an old saying: Let me be the person that my dog thinks I am. I would like to change that to say: Let me be the agility handler that my dog wants me to be. Remember these guidelines every time you take your dog out to play, and you will be that handler.

3
Readiness Tests

A few years ago, I interviewed a group of experienced agility handlers about how their training had changed from their first to subsequent dogs. Virtually everyone said that they no longer hurried. They reported that they focused on extensive foundation work before they started obstacle work. Next, they taught the individual obstacles to the highest level of performance before they proceeded to sequences. Then they spent plenty of time on short sequences before they moved on to longer sequences.

Given the addictive nature of agility, it is hard to resist asking too much of your dog too quickly. At each stage, he should master a topnotch performance before he proceeds to something more difficult. This will keep him confident, and it will minimize the chances of having to fix a problem later, which may or may not be successful.

In this chapter, I provide a series of activities to assist you in evaluating your dog's current skill level. We will start with a review of foundation skills. Then I'll describe a series of exercises that you can do on the agility field to make sure that your pup is ready to tackle intermediate challenges. If he is ready to go on, great. If not, be patient. A few extra weeks on the basics will pay off in the long term.

Foundation Skills Checklist

Before you ask more from your pup or dog, you should be able to answer in the affirmative to each of the following skills on page 24, which should be performed in both a familiar setting and a new setting with distractions. (Distractions should include dogs running nearby.)

There are other foundation skills that some trainers would call essential. For example, Susan Garrett, well-known author, teacher, and competitor, strongly recommends that dogs learn to race from a *stay* position to a left-side or right-side *heel* without passing you. This reinforces the *recall*, of course, but also teaches the dog how to switch from running to collection. Other trainers encourage clicker training, touching a target, and playing interactively with you and

Foundation Skill	Able to Perform in a Familiar Setting	Able to Perform in a New Setting With Distractions	Comments
Your dog comes to you reliably even if other dogs are running loose within 50 yards (45.5 m).			When dogs are competing in agility, there are often dogs running in a nearby ring or exercising in an adjacent field.
Your dog walks nicely on both sides.			Teaching your dog to walk on a loose lead next to you is both an issue of comfort and one of relationship building. A dog who drags you along is in charge and is unlikely to work with you on the agility field.
Your dog can sit and lie down quickly.			These two basic obedience commands are important because they are required on the table obstacle.
Your dog will stay until released in any setting, including when facing jumps and tunnels.			Agility courses are often designed to require a start line *stay*.
Off lead, your dog can run with you in a large circle (15- to 20-foot [4.5- to 6-m] diameter) in both directions and remain on the outside of the curve near your leg.			To steer your dog in agility, he must understand that it is his job to run the outside of any curve rather than ducking behind you.
Your dog has a *release* command, which tells him that he can move from the start line or off a contact obstacle.			To control a dog on course, the dog must stop when asked and stay in that spot until told that he can go on.
Your dog has learned games that teach him to read your body language.			Great foundation games include teaching your dog to back up, weave through your legs, turn 180 degrees, and turn right and left.
Your dog has learned the behavior you want in the contact zone on the A-frame and dogwalk.			Before your dog is allowed to perform the A-frame and dogwalk, you need to teach the behavior that will guarantee that he touches the contact zone. This may include several methods, such as the two on/two off or four off.
Your dog has fun working with you.			Agility played well requires a dog who is full of joy about getting to play with you.

Before tackling intermediate agility, a dog must be able to sit and lie down quickly.

a toy. Some trainers teach their dogs good balance by using tools such as a wobble board. The bottom line is that the more you teach your dog, if it is done positively and without overwhelming him, the more you develop his brain for future learning.

Agility Skills Checklist
Next, let's take a look at your dog's agility skills to see if he's ready to move on to the intermediate level.

Test #1: Obstacles on a Curve
The first test evaluates your dog's ability to perform obstacles set on a curve. It is the application of the circle running exercise you practiced earlier.

Setup	Test Your Dog	Desired Behavior
See Figure 3.1 for the configuration of obstacles.	Stand in the middle of the circle and direct your dog to run around in both directions.	Your dog should run around the curve performing each obstacle. He should be running at his fastest speed with enthusiasm. He should be able to do this in both directions.

Readiness Tests

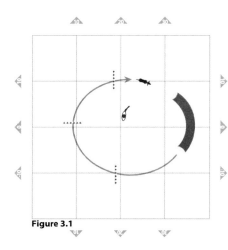

Figure 3.1

If your dog flies around the circle in both directions performing each obstacle in sequence, you both get a gold star—your dog understands and enjoys the game.

If your pup misses obstacles, you need to return to rewarding him for individual obstacles. Send him over one jump, click while he is jumping, and toss his toy or a hunk of cookie ahead of him. When he likes that game, add a second obstacle. Alternate between rewarding for one jump and then for two jumps. Gradually build to the full circle.

If your dog is slow, you need to do work to motivate him. Remember, during this and other exercises, that you should surprise your dog by tossing your toy or a hunk of cookie intermittently rather than rewarding him only at the end of each run. This will keep him interested and optimistic.

Test #2: Driving Ahead

The second exercise will evaluate your dog's ability to drive ahead of you and look for the next obstacle. Agility courses are composed of obstacles set in lines and on curves, so your pup must understand that he can keep moving forward. Otherwise, he will be limited by your speed, which is rarely a good thing.

Setup	Test Your Dog	Desired Behavior
Set up two jumps. For big dogs, position the jumps 10 to 15 feet (3 to 4.5 m) apart. For small dogs, set the jumps 10 feet (3 m) apart.	Put your target out past the second jump. This can be a toy or another target, such as cookies in a plastic bottle. Let your dog see the target. Then run him back behind the first jump and quickly turn around. Give him your *go* command to send him over the jumps. Make sure that you move forward as he runs, and reinforce him with a game or cookie at the end. Now repeat the game without the lure. If your dog continues to drive over both jumps, reinforce him by tossing a toy or cookie past the second jump.	When facing a line of obstacles, your dog should understand that it is his job to keep running ahead and taking the next one if you tell him to.

Results

If your dog runs straight ahead over the jumps to the target, give yourselves a gold star. Teaching a dog to drive ahead of you is one of the most challenging aspects of agility. It is worthwhile to build this game up to three or more jumps, but you can do this while you begin other intermediate skills.

Hooked on Agility

Alternating the *Heel*
Although you want a dog who can walk next to you nicely when asked, it is also important that he understands that sometimes you want him to go ahead. You can teach him that both behaviors are important by alternating the formal *heel* with opportunities for him to walk or run ahead of you as long as he doesn't drag you along.

On the other hand, you may have a dog who wants to look at you all the time. In real life, this is a nice trait, but it creates problems in agility. Dogs with excessive handler focus complete one obstacle and then curve back toward the handler or try to run while looking back. The result is that the dog misses the subsequent obstacle. This is particularly common with people-oriented breeds, such as Labrador Retrievers, and with herding breeds that want to loop back and round you up. If your dog does more than glance at you or misses the second jump, take more time at this level before you go on to longer sequences. Here are your steps to teach the *go* command:

1. Show him the target. Then take him by the collar and gently lead him back behind the first jump. Release him. He should take the jump and run to the target. Go out and reward him with a second cookie. When he is confident with one jump, add the second. His focus should be forward and not on you.
2. Gradually fade the target. You can continue to reinforce your pup by tossing his toy or a hunk of cookie after he commits to taking the second jump.

Test #3: Contact Obstacles and Contact Zones
The third test is to determine whether your dog understands the performance you want on the contact obstacles.

Setup	Test Your Dog	Desired Behavior
Use a full-height A-frame and dogwalk.	Send your dog up and over each contact obstacle three times. Each time, ask for the contact performance you have decided on. Do not lure him into position with a cookie, but you may reward him for the correct behavior. Test each of the contact obstacles separately.	Your dog should perform the contact behavior each time in the same way. For example, he should stop in a two on/two off, run down through the contact zone, or lie down after he completes the obstacle.

Results
If your dog nails his contact each time you send him over the obstacle, you both get another gold star. If he misses the contact zone, does something different each time, or relies on you to lure him into position, he is not ready to go on. Remember that your hands should stay out of your pocket or bag until your dog gets the correct behavior. Anything else amounts to bribery, and your goal is to teach your dog to do an independent contact.

Test whether your dog understands the performance you want on the contact obstacles.

Learning to touch the contact zone consistently in practice and at trials is an ongoing challenge for every agility handler. In Chapter 22, I will share the changing world of teaching contacts. Many trainers are trying new methods since I wrote *The Beginner's Guide to Dog Agility*. Whatever method you choose, it is well worth your time to teach the behavior thoroughly and then continue to reinforce it throughout your dog's career.

Dogs should not be allowed to do contacts in a sequence until they can perform the contact obstacle by itself exactly as you want.

Test #4: Contact Obstacles and Speed

This test adds the element of speed to the contact performance. (Proceed only if your dog received a gold star in Test #3.)

Setup	Test Your Dog	Desired Behavior
Use a full-height A-frame and dogwalk. Add two jumps before the contact.	Send your dog over one jump and then up and over a contact obstacle three times. Each time, ask for the contact performance you have decided on. Do not lure him into position with a cookie, but you may reward him for the correct behavior. If your dog is successful, send him over two jumps before the contact. This will increase his speed over the A-frame and dogwalk. Test each of the contact obstacles separately with the addition of jumps.	Even though he is going faster, your dog should perform the contact behavior each time in the same way. For example, he should stop in a two on/ two off, run down through the contact zone, or lie down after he completes the obstacle.

Results

When you add more obstacles and increase speed, you may find that your dog can't do what you thought he could. For example, a student's Labrador Retriever seemed to have mastered his two on/two off until we

added one jump. The minute he accelerated from jump to A-frame, it was clear that he had not yet learned the self-control necessary to consistently stop in the contact zone. Rather than adding more obstacles to the sequence and letting him make mistakes, we worked with him with two obstacles until that performance was perfect. I stood right at the bottom of the A-frame facing the dog as he ran down. My presence gave him a reason to slow down. When he stopped in his two on/two off contact, I reinforced him with a cookie. This exercise showed him the self-control required to stop. As soon as he understood that, I got out of the way. Once he could perform one jump and stop in the two on/two off on his own, we were able to add a second jump fairly quickly.

Test #5: Teeter

Although the teeter is one of the contact obstacles, I have isolated it because the movement of this obstacle can become a source of concern for some dogs. It makes sense to train it slowly and methodically, never moving to the next height until your dog is completely confident.

Setup	Test Your Dog	Desired Behavior
Use a teeter set with a drop of approximately 12 inches (30.5 cm).	Send your dog over the teeter three times. Each time, ask for the contact performance you have decided on. Do not lure him into position with a cookie, but you may reward him for the correct behavior.	Your dog should race up to the end of the teeter confidently and perform the contact behavior each time in the same way.
	If he is successful, send him over one jump and onto the teeter. If that goes well, add a second jump before the contact.	Even though he is going faster, your dog should continue to perform the teeter confidently and correctly.
If your dog passes these two tests with flying colors, raise the teeter one height. Never go beyond the point at which your dog is comfortable.	Ask him to perform the teeter at the new height without and then with jumps.	At each new height, your dog should be excited to play this game and be able to perform the way you want.

Make sure that you are clear about the contact performance you want. Your options are four on (all four feet on the teeter), two on/two off, and even a *down* at the end.

Results

From this test, you will determine the correct level for your dog to work the teeter. Any sign of anxiety means that you have gone one step too far.

All of the exercises in this book should be done with the teeter at the correct level for your dog's developmental stage. If he is working at lower than full height, continue to work the teeter separately and gradually increase the height.

Test #6: Weave Poles

The other obstacle that requires a slow, methodical process is the weaves. For this book, I am assuming that your dog has, at a minimum, progressed to performing a straight line of weave poles with guides on and can find the entry if you approach the weaves straight on.

Setup	Test Your Dog	Desired Behavior
Set up 12 weaves. Put on as many guide wires as your dog needs.	Take your dog back about 10 feet (3 m). Send him to the poles. Hesitate in order to give him a moment to find the entry, and then move up to his head until he exits. Repeat with your dog on your other side.	Your dog should enter the weaves on his own from either side. He should remain in the poles from end to end. He should move as quickly as he is capable of rather than walking through the poles.

Results

If your dog is not yet weaving independently without guides, you should continue to work this obstacle in addition to the exercises in this book. If your dog is doing well with the wires, start removing them one by one. However, never be afraid to put them back on briefly during practice if your dog backslides or if you encounter a tough weave pole entry as part of a sequence.

In Chapter 14, we will teach your dog to enter the weave poles correctly from a variety of angles.

If your dog has any problems with the table, break the behavior down and retrain.

Setup	Test Your Dog	Desired Behavior
Use a regulation-sized table.	Send your dog to the table three times. Do not lure him onto the table, but you may reward him for the correct behavior.	Your dog should race directly to the table without slowing down.
	If he is successful, send him to the table and have him sit.	Your dog should sit without hesitation.
	Next, send him to the table and have him down.	Your dog should down without hesitation.
	If he is successful so far, repeat both the *sit* and *down* and have your pup hold each position for five seconds.	Your dog should hold either position and wait to be released from the table.

Test #7: Table

The table is a seemingly straightforward obstacle for dogs to perform. In reality, there are three distinct parts that the dog must master: running to and getting onto the table, sitting or lying down, and holding that position until excused. One sees many dogs eating up precious seconds by slowing down on the way to the table because it means a break in the game, taking forever to sit or lie down, or leaping up before the time is up. Some dogs have taught their handlers to do amazing contortions to get them into the correct position.

Results

From this test, you will determine your dog's comfort with all three aspects of performing the table. If he reveals any issues, break the behavior down and retrain. For example, if your dog is slow going to the table, play a game in which you and he race to the table for a cookie party. Skip the *sit* or *down* until he loves getting onto the obstacle. Then add the other elements. The table makes a great bad-weather-day game in the house. My dogs love to race each other to the table to see who can earn the cookie by sitting or lying down first.

Concluding Thoughts

If your dog nailed these readiness tests, let's get going with your new skills. In Part II, we will launch right into 12 strategies you can use to get yourself and your dog ready to run in an intermediate sequence.

Part II
Intermediate Handling Skills

In this section, I will introduce you to 12 intermediate skills. It may seem like a lot when you get into the details of each skill, so keep in mind that learning to do these well with your dog is a long-term commitment. When starting a young dog, I think in terms of at least a year of practice until we are comfortable working together through a beginning sequence and at least another six months before we can tackle an intermediate sequence with speed and precision. One of the best things about agility is that you can continue to improve forever. Working on these skills keeps me going to class week after week after more than a dozen years in the game.

In teaching you to perform these skills, I have tried to present a sequential plan for you to follow. This always makes me a bit anxious for one simple reason: All dogs are individuals. No single plan will work with all dogs. For example, in the first skill, which focuses on handling your dog from a distance, I say that you should work to handle him from 8 to 10 feet (2.5 to 3 m) off to the side of the obstacle. In reality, with an insecure dog, it may be terrific to get 6 feet (2 m) away. It is important to set high standards for your dog, but adjust any of the exercises to match reality. Some dogs may also progress faster than you expect. I just came in from playing with my nine-month-old Border Collie. She has a solid foundation of jumping at a low height, but I had never asked her to jump a complete pinwheel with four jumps before. Within a few minutes, she was able to go through all five steps of the pinwheel jumping exercise. With a dog like this, you will need to adjust the exercises in a different way so that he is challenged appropriately. The bottom line is that you should modify any exercise to make it work for your dog.

Within each chapter, you will find many exercises that you can set up for your dog if you have equipment. In many cases, you can make do with jumps, a tunnel, a table, and weave poles. At the end of each chapter, there is a longer sequence that puts the skill into context. If you can set it up and practice, great. If you can't, mental practice is a powerful tool. Before we get started, here are two important training notes:

1. **Behavior Reinforcement:** As you know, you can reinforce your dog's behavior with cookies or interactive play. In the chapters that follow, I will often tell you to give your dog a cookie. You can substitute interactive play, such as a game of tug, for cookies at any time. Ideally, you will alternate between food reinforcement and play to keep your dog energized.

2. **Delivery of Cookies:** You may find that if you give your dog cookies from your hands when you want to reward him, he gets obsessed with looking at you. This is not good because it keeps him from focusing forward at the next obstacle. You can prevent this by tossing the cookie onto the ground and letting your dog race to get it. If you train on grass, use something white, such as string cheese, so that he can easily see it.

Let's get started on your intermediate skills!

4
Lateral Distance

During the first months of agility, when their dogs are becoming comfortable with the obstacles, handlers often get in the habit of escorting them to each obstacle. The problem with handling this way is that it is very limiting. It does not allow you to front cross effectively or pull your dog toward the next obstacle efficiently. In addition, if your dog is speedy, it also causes you to fall farther and farther behind, which limits your communication.

In this chapter, we will focus on teaching your dog to work laterally (off to the side). Once you teach him to take obstacles while you are 5 or 10 feet (1.5 or 3 m) or even farther away, you will be poised to improve other skills that will follow. Many high-level agility dogs are capable of working laterally at a distance that simply takes my breath away. Even dogs who seem dependent on their handler's proximity can learn to handle obstacles more independently than you might imagine if you proceed sequentially.

We will tackle two different exercises in which we will teach your dog to work off to the side. The first will focus on handling a pinwheel from a lateral distance. The second will highlight handling a line of jumps from a position well off to the side. This exact process can and should be used to teach your dog to perform every obstacle without your hovering around him.

Prerequisite Skills
The only prerequisite to begin teaching your dog to work farther away from you is that he can perform a series of jumps in a circle or a straight line of jumps. In the previous chapter, you tested your dog's ability to do exactly that.

Teaching the Pinwheel
Whenever dogs must handle jumps set in a circle or a partial circle, that configuration is called a pinwheel. Pinwheels can include other obstacles too, but a series of jumps is the classic setup.

Pinwheels are the perfect place to start your lateral work because you have already had your dog do lots of circle jumping so that he recognizes the pattern. To practice, set up four jumps to form a circle. The diameter should be such that your dog can run around comfortably rather than feeling overly constricted. Bring out a toy your dog loves, a food bag, or a cookie-filled plastic bottle that he will chase. It is essential that you have something to throw to reward your dog for working away from you. I will refer to all these objects as a "toy."

Your goal in this exercise is to teach your dog to run around the circle taking each jump while you remain in the center, a minimum of 10 feet (3 m) away. We will proceed through a series of steps that will show your dog how to do exactly that.

Step 1

1. Start with the dog on your right. Stay as close as you usually stay to him. Hold your toy in your left hand. This is very important because you want your "steering hand" empty. Send him over the first jump, and move forward as you would normally.

2. As soon as he jumps, toss his toy onto the path to the second jump but not over the second jump. (See Photo 4.A. and Figure 4.1.) When he gets to the toy, run out and play or reinforce with a cookie. Make sure to reinforce on the path rather than moving away from that spot before you offer a cookie or game. This sends a clear message that you like it when your pup goes to that place.

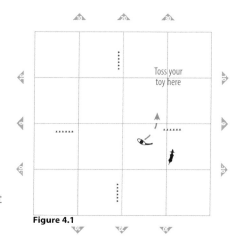

Toss your toy here

Figure 4.1

4.A: As soon as your dog jumps, toss his toy on the path to the second jump but not over the second jump.

Intermediate Handling Skills

3.

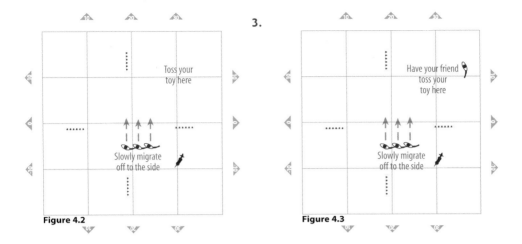

Figure 4.2

Figure 4.3

Repeat this game several times. Very slowly migrate off to the side so that you are getting closer to the center of the circle. Each time, toss your toy onto the path to the next obstacle. If you toss too short and the dog has to curve in to get it, that is counterproductive because it teaches him to come to you rather than helping him understand that you like it when he stays off to the side. (See Figure 4.2.)

4. If your dog wants to pull in toward you rather than jumping because you are holding something he wants, recruit a friend. Have her stand outside the circle and toss the toy onto your dog's path after he commits to the jump. (See Figure 4.3.)

If at any time during this exercise, your dog is reluctant to jump at all, you can lure him by tossing the toy early over the jump a few times. But ultimately, the toy toss should be timed to land after your dog has jumped so that it serves as reinforcement.

Step 2

It's time to add the second jump once your dog is comfortable taking one jump with you at least 10 feet (3 m) to the side. Your toy should be in your left hand as before. If you hold a toy in front of a dog's face, he will have trouble paying attention to where he is going.

Jump Heights

Remember that dogs less than a year old should not jump higher than their elbow. Some veterinarians suggest that dogs not jump until their growth plates close. Growth plates close for dogs with an adult weight of less than 50 pounds (22.5 kg) by 9 to 12 months. For dogs with an adult weight estimated at more than 50 pounds (22.5 kg), growth plates close at 10 to 14 months. The exercises in this chapter can be done safely and effectively with young dogs with the jump bars on the ground.

Lateral Distance

4.B

4.B: Cue the second jump, and toss your toy on the path between the second and the third jump

1. Start by sending your dog over the first jump from your lateral position, and continue to move forward.
2. Cue the second jump, and toss your toy onto the path between the second and the third jump. (See Photo 4.B.) As before, you may lure him a couple of times by tossing before he jumps, but then try to time your toss to reinforce him after he clears the second jump. If you have trouble getting the toy to land in the correct spot, bring your friend back to toss the toy from the outside of the circle. Having the toy land in the correct spot is essential for this process to work. (See Figure 4.4.)

Once you develop the ability to handle with some lateral distance from your dog, the use of your arm changes. In the past, I emphasized that you should carry your cueing arm relatively close to your body. This was because a raised arm should tell your dog that you want him to travel on a path at a distance from you and take the obstacles he encounters. Now is the time that you will start lifting your arm to tell your dog to work away from you. (See Photo 4.C.) As you cue him to jump in the circle, raise your arm to approximately shoulder level. Keep your arm elevated as you work around the circle.

If your dog has trouble with the second jump, you may need to move closer to that jump a couple of times and then migrate away as you did before. If he goes around the second jump to get to the toy, you may want to put several cookies into a plastic bottle and use it as your toy. This is a great tool because the dog simply won't get rewarded if he makes an "error." But when he gets it right, you can open the bottle and reward him profusely.

Step 3

Repeat the same process as in Step 2 for the third jump. This time, the toy should be tossed onto the dog's path between the third and fourth jump.

Step 4

Repeat the same process as in Step 3 for the fourth jump, which will complete the circle.

Step 5

Next, reverse direction so that your dog is working on your left hand. As you remember, dogs must

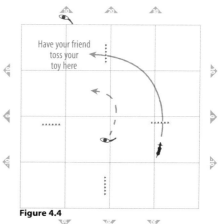

Have your friend toss your toy here

Figure 4.4

Intermediate Handling Skills

be able to perform every agility exercise on your left hand and your right hand with equal comfort. Your toy will be in your right hand so that your dog isn't distracted by it as he runs. You may need to go through the first four steps again, but they will progress more quickly.

Step 6

When your dog is able to successfully jump around the circle while you maintain your lateral distance, gradually fade the toss of the toy or cookie.

4.C: Lift your arm to tell your dog to work away from you.

Start to reinforce intermittently with verbal praise. Don't do this too fast, though, or your dog may lose his drive forward. Surprise him with the toy intermittently to keep him energetic while playing this game.

Take Note
Three or four repetitions of one exercise are plenty for any given lesson.

Teaching Jumps in a Line

The next challenge is to teach your dog to take jumps or other obstacles that are set in a line while you handle well off to the side. Over time, you can expect to stay 10 feet (3 m) or even farther to the side while you cue your dog to jump or perform another obstacle. As with the pinwheel, this skill is essential so that you can get into a good position to cue your dog when there is a change of direction.

Because your dog already has significant experience going over a straight line of jumps at the novice level, this exercise should proceed fairly easily. As with the pinwheel, the precision of your toy delivery is very important, so invite an agility friend over and alternate tossing for each other.

To prepare for this exercise, set up two jumps to a table in a straight line. The distance between jumps should be comfortable for your dog. A toy dog might like 10 feet (3 m), and a dog with a big stride might prefer 15 feet (4.5 m).

Step 1

1. Put a cookie onto the table. It's okay if your dog sees it unless it makes him lose his mind.
2. Put him on a *stay* behind the first jump. Lead out between the first and the second jump.
3. Release your dog and send him over the jumps, handling him from your typical lateral distance. (See Photo 4.D.) Remember to move forward.
4. Let him jump onto the table and eat his cookie. If your dog races around the jumps to get to

the table or breaks his *stay*, have your friend stand to the side and toss the cookie onto the table after your dog commits to the table. (See Figure 4.5.)

5. Then repeat the exercise several times while you migrate laterally in small increments. (See Photo 4.E.) Run parallel to the jumps and the table as your dog does his job. (See Figure 4.6.)

As you did during the pinwheel exercise, your arm should stay elevated to shoulder level to communicate that you want him to continue working while he maintains his distance from you.

If at any point your dog starts curving in toward you rather than driving forward, you have moved away from the obstacles too quickly or asked him to travel too far. In the first case, migrate away from him in smaller increments, and make sure that the cookie you are using is a high-value reward so that he thinks about it more than you. In the second case, shorten the exercise to one jump. Add a second jump when your dog is comfortable with driving over them to his toy.

Step 2

Gradually fade the target on the table when your dog is clearly enjoying the game of running to the table, regardless of your distance. If he drives ahead while you maintain your lateral position without the cookie lure on the table, toss cookies to him once he gets onto the table.

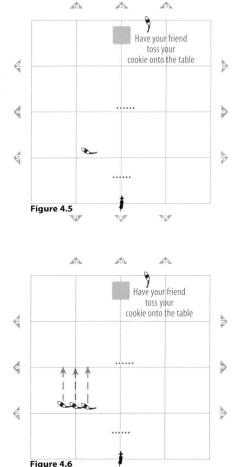

Figure 4.5

Figure 4.6

Step 3

Use the same process to build lateral distance from all of the obstacles, including the dogwalk and A-frame.

Lateral Distance Issues

Beware of a phenomenon I often observe with my students. They will start out with significant lateral distance. But as they move past the first jump, the jump magnet sucks them back in to their usual distance from the obstacle. Do your best to maintain a consistent lateral distance around the pinwheel. Ask your training partner to watch whether you stay away and handle laterally or rush toward your dog.

Intermediate Handling Skills

4.D: Release your dog and send him over the jumps, handling him from your typical lateral distance.
4.E: Migrate laterally in small increments.

Mental Practice

Figure 4.7 combines a pinwheel and a straight-line exercise. After you get your dog started over jump #1, imagine handling it with good lateral distance. What is the advantage of handling this sequence laterally?

Answer: The correct answer is that using lateral distance allows you to keep up with your dog because he will run much faster than you. Rather than trying to steer from his tail, you will be able to direct his head, which is always more powerful.

Concluding Thoughts

Once you are freed from escorting your dog to each obstacle, you can then focus on positioning yourself correctly to tell him where to go next. In fact, you will use lateral distance work extensively in other intermediate skills that follow, such as the front cross and shoulder pull. The bottom line is that lateral distance is the single skill that allows you to cut corners so that you can keep up with your dog at all.

Students often ask if we can work on lateral distance. But once your dog becomes comfortable with the idea of having you direct him from off to the side, you can practice this skill on almost any sequence. Rather than running close to every obstacle, get in the habit of choosing sections of each sequence that you will handle laterally.

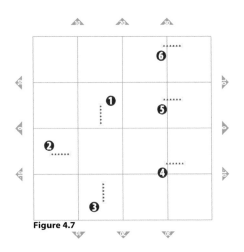

Figure 4.7

Lateral Distance

5
Changing Speeds

This chapter covers one of the most underestimated communication tools in agility: the ability of the handler to change speed when traveling around the course. By simply learning to speed up or slow down at key points on a course, handlers have the power to tell their dogs whether to run full speed ahead or to collect and prepare for a tight turn. Naturally, our dogs must be taught to "read" our speed changes, but they do this relatively easily given their superb ability to read and react to human body language.

At the novice level in agility, most handlers move at a constant rate of speed. When learning the sport, folks might slow down a bit as their dog gets on the dogwalk or enters the weave poles, but other than that, the tendency is to pick a speed and stick to it. To enter the intermediate ranks, you must learn to accelerate and decelerate consciously so that your dog understands what is coming on course. If you and your dog don't master this skill, he will burn up precious seconds with very wide turns.

Learning to use speed changes strategically while running a course is a relatively recent change in agility. Experienced handlers have used speed changes without thinking about it for years, but a new understanding has translated into more efficient handling and faster course times.

Prerequisite Skills

Before you and your dog tackle the intermediate skill of changing speeds, he should be able to perform novice-level sequences that include both jumps and tunnels. The sequences can be relatively short, as few as four obstacles, or longer, depending on your dog's level of expertise.

Understanding Speed Changes

Most agility sequences or courses have a section where the obstacles are set in a line or on a curve and the dog simply needs to run forward to take the next obstacle he encounters. These delightful sections are the racetracks of agility. Figure 5.1 is a straightforward sequence that calls for the dog to go full out.

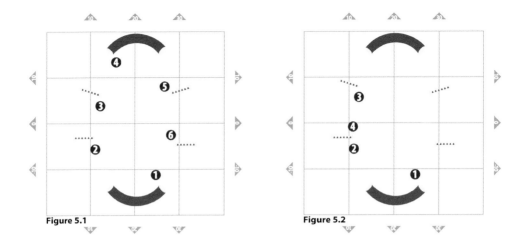

Figure 5.1   Figure 5.2

When you are faced with a line of obstacles like this, you can communicate to your dog that you want him to race forward by increasing your own speed. He will learn that any time you accelerate forward, he should put it in gear and drive ahead, taking whatever obstacles he sees.

Then there are those places on course where the dog needs to dramatically change direction. When you encounter a place where your dog needs to make a sharp turn, you can communicate to him, by decreasing your own speed, that he is going to need to collect himself so that he can turn efficiently. He will learn that any time you decelerate, he should prepare to go in a new direction. You will find directional changes increasingly common on intermediate courses compared with those you encountered in the novice ranks.

It is important to know what happens when we ask our dogs to change directions. To prepare for a turn of some sort, your dog needs to shorten his stride. (See Photo 5.A.) This is known as "collection" in the horse world. Collection allows a dog to turn tightly in the new

5.A: To prepare for a turn, the dog needs to shorten his stride.
5.B: If the dog does not collect himself to prepare for a turn, he will take several extra strides forward.

Intermediate Handling Skills

direction. If a dog does not collect himself to prepare for a turn, he will take several extra strides forward. (See Photo 5.B.) This will result in a wide, time-consuming turn or a disqualifying off course if he takes the obvious but incorrect obstacle straight ahead. Figure 5.2 is an example of a sequence where collection is required. As you can see, the dog needs to wrap around the stanchion of jump #3 to pull back to jump #4.

You can see how easy it would be for the dog who didn't receive advance warning about the turn to blast straight ahead into the tunnel. That is what will happen if you continue racing forward at the same speed until you get close to jump #3. Deceleration is the communication tool you will use any time you want to pull your dog toward you. It will work on a 180-degree turn like the one on this map and is also invaluable on 90-degree turns where you need to pull your dog toward you. Dogs must be taught how to read your deceleration—*hey, there must be a turn coming*—and also how to collect themselves. We will be working on those skills in this chapter.

In regard to speed changes, there is one important distinction that sometimes confuses people. With the use of acceleration, both handler and dog are accelerating. Ideally, the dog reads the handler's acceleration and runs ahead to find the next obstacle. However, when we are talking about deceleration, only the handler is decelerating.

We are not asking our dogs to decelerate. We are asking them to collect themselves very briefly by shortening their stride while maintaining as much speed as possible. Said another way, handler acceleration should cue dog acceleration. Handler deceleration should cue dog collection.

Let's look at a sequence (see Figure 5.3) on which the handler should accelerate to drive the dog forward on certain sections and then decelerate to cue the turns on other sections. Identify how you would cue your dog by changing your speed.

If you said that you would accelerate on obstacles #1 through #5, you are right—this

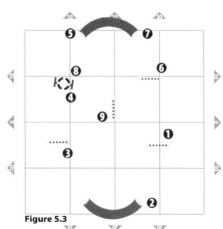

Figure 5.3

Changing Speeds

section is a racetrack. If you said that you would decelerate before jump #6 and front cross to pull the dog back toward the tunnel, a gold star for you. After the dog emerges from the tunnel, it is time to decelerate again. By slowing down before the tire, you will cue your dog that there is a turn from the tire to the #9 jump. If you were to blast past the tire before cueing a turn, the odds are very high that you would send your dog back over jump #3.

Teaching Body Language Changes

Most intermediate and advanced courses include combinations of obstacles that are ideally handled with multiple speed changes. With a bit of training, you can teach your dog simple, consistent cues that communicate whether he should accelerate or collect in preparation for a turn. Dogs should not have to work too hard to decipher subtle differences.

Tracy Sklenar, agility competitor, teacher, and author, describes the body language cues you can use to communicate with your dog in an article in *Dog Sport Magazine*.

The Language of Acceleration

Tracy writes that it is essential to use your whole body. (See Photo 5.C.) Run on the balls of your feet so that you tip forward slightly. Drive with your arms. Lengthen your stride. Watch your dog out of the corner of your eye as you sprint. One image that may help is thinking about how you might look if you were a track star racing to the finish line. This body language will help drive your dog forward by encouraging him to extend.

The Language of Deceleration

The transition from acceleration to deceleration should provide a dramatic cue to the dog that a change in direction is coming. Again, get your whole body involved. Stand up straight and take shorter steps. (See Photo 5.D.) In some cases where you near a tight turn, you may even lean back a bit. Let your arms keep moving, but don't pump as hard. Keep your eyes on your dog. The change of posture between acceleration and deceleration should look dramatically different to your dog so that he can react.

5.C: To accelerate, get your whole body involved.
5.D: To decelerate, stand up straight and take shorter steps.

Intermediate Handling Skills

Practicing Acceleration and Deceleration Without Your Dog

It is wise to perfect your speed changes before involving and potentially confusing your dog. First, practice sprinting without the obstacles, and practice the clear body language that Tracy described in the previous section. Then set up a sequence of obstacles that require only acceleration—Figure 5.1 in this chapter will work perfectly. Practice running that sequence at top speed. It is likely to feel very different than what you have been doing, so repeat until you feel comfortable.

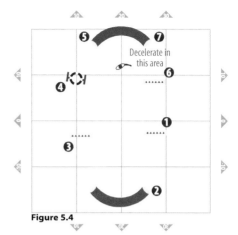

Figure 5.4

Next practice a sequence with changes of direction that require you to decelerate. The timing on your deceleration will vary widely, depending on your dog. If your dog is high drive, you will start to decelerate farther back from the obstacle than if your dog works more closely to you. In each case, though, the deceleration should happen before you reach the obstacle that precedes the turn. If you run past the obstacle and then slow down, there is no possibility for a tight turn. In the sequence shown in Figure 5.4, you are slowing down, decelerating before obstacle #6 to communicate the tight turn back to the tunnel #7 entry.

Teaching Your Dog to Accelerate

Now we will add your dog to the mix. I am making an assumption that you have already taught your dog to take every obstacle directly in his path if you keep moving forward. The difference here is that you are going to open up and really run. Don't include contact obstacles initially because these may require you to stop to get the correct behaviors. You can add the contacts later when you are comfortable with the two speed changes.

One important note in teaching acceleration is that it matters where you reinforce your dog. Because you are asking him to drive forward at full speed, make sure to toss a toy or cookie ahead of him when you want to reward. This tells him you like it when he is driving an obvious line of jumps. If you reward from your hands, you are teaching him to come back to you. If you find running like an Olympic sprinter and tossing too challenging, bring your friend out again and have her toss the toy or cookie onto the dog's path.

To teach your dog to accelerate, use the straightforward sequence on which you have already practiced. (Refer to Figure 5.1.)

Step 1

Once you release your dog, run as fast as you can through the sequence. Continue to look at each obstacle and cue it with your hand so that your dog knows that you want him to complete them. If your dog gets so excited by the increase in your energy and change in your body language that he skips obstacles, slow down just a bit until he completes everything, and then gradually speed up. Most dogs visibly enjoy permission to run full out once they understand that it is okay.

Step 2
If at any point your dog gets ahead of you, throw your arm forward (as if you are slapping him on the bottom) and give your obstacle commands quickly so that he knows it is okay to keep going.

Step 3
If you get ahead of your dog, which is likely at the tunnel, don't wait around for him to come out. Take off running once he has entered. Many handlers can get out past jump #3 if they keep sprinting. Remember to run looking back over your shoulder at your dog and indicate the obstacle with your hand. If you simply turn your back on your dog, he will skip obstacles to catch up. If you walk the sequences carefully beforehand, you will know exactly where you are going, and you can manage to run and watch your dog too.

Teaching Your Dog to Decelerate and Wrap
Teaching deceleration is a bit more technical than acceleration. There are two goals in this work. First, you will teach your dog how to collect himself and wrap tightly around a jump stanchion. In fact, you will start to see him banking like a plane in the air while he is jumping. Then you will teach him how to read your deceleration as a cue that a change of direction is coming so that he can collect himself in preparation for the tight turn.

Step 1
1. Set your dog up facing a jump at a slight angle. (See Photo 5.E.) Position him just a few feet (m) from the jump. You don't want much speed initially. Position yourself facing the stanchion with just enough space for your dog to get in front of you. Put a cookie in your hand farthest from your dog. Cue your dog over the jump using the hand closest to your dog. (See Photo 5.F.) Once he commits to taking the jump, lower the cookie so that he wraps around the stanchion to get it. (See Photo 5.G.) Your dog may land straight a few times and then curve toward you, but most dogs learn to arc in the air fairly quickly. After all, they want to get to the cookie as fast as possible.
2. Repeat several times at the same distance until he is comfortably collecting himself. You will notice that he will be landing on the ground much more softly once he gets the idea of collection.
3. Move him back from the jump very gradually. (See Photo 5.H.) When he can start from at least 10 feet (3 m) back and still wrap tightly around the stanchion, you are ready for the next step.

Step 2
At this level, you will work on teaching your dog to wrap with a bit more speed.
1. Add a second jump. (See Photo 5.I.) Position your dog behind both jumps and lead out.
2. As you release him and direct him to take both jumps, move to the position at the stanchion

Intermediate Handling Skills

5.E: Set your dog up facing the jump.
5.F: Cue your dog to jump.
5.G: Lower the cookie to wrap him around the stanchion.
5.H: Move him back gradually.

that you used in Step I. Have your cookie ready, and offer it to your dog for wrapping in front of you. (See Photo 5.J.)

Step 3

Now you will start to add your speed change to cue the wrap.
1. Rather than leading out, start with your dog.
2. As you approach the second jump, slow down. Continue to use your hand cue to tell your dog that he should travel forward to the jump. You won't make it to the stanchion, but rotate to face your dog as you have been doing as soon as he has committed to the jump.

Your dog will recognize this move and curve toward you. Reinforce that with a cookie. Fairly quickly, most dogs start to recognize that the deceleration is the cue to pull back toward you after they have jumped. Timing is important here. If your dog curves into you before the jump, you rotated before he had committed. Hesitate just a bit longer until you know that he is going to take

Changing Speeds

5.I: Add a second jump.
5.J: Move to the stanchion and reward your dog for wrapping tightly.

the jump. You will be able to observe your dog's understanding of collection by the tightness of his turns on the two-jump exercise.

Step 4
1. When you are pleased with your dog's ability to wrap around the stanchion, start adding additional obstacles. Each new obstacle will add to his speed, so you might find that you need to decelerate earlier than before to keep him from driving straight ahead.
2. Continue to reinforce with cookies as he bends around the stanchion.

Step 5
Next it is time to combine your skills of acceleration and deceleration.
1. Set up a sequence such as Figure 5.3 in this chapter to practice.
2. If your dog gets amped up by the fast sections and forgets to read your deceleration as a tight wrap, bring your cookies out and reinforce the message of the speed change.

Step 6
Now it's time to combine your dog's understanding of lateral distance and deceleration. Putting these two skills together will be essential for mastering an intermediate-level shoulder pull and

The Ultimate Deceleration
There are times when you will not only slow down but actually come to a brief but complete standstill. This is used when you must tell your dog, in a dramatic fashion, that he needs to collect himself and come toward you. (We will discuss this in more detail when we get to the subject of obstacle discrimination in Chapter 12.) A quick stop is often used to cue a dog to take an obstacle that is closest to the handler when there are two obstacles placed very close together.

Intermediate Handling Skills

front cross, which we will discuss in the next two chapters.

1. Return to your lateral distance exercises from Chapter 4. As you send your dog around the pinwheel or down a line of jumps from a lateral position, decelerate to pull him tightly around the last jump or any jump that you select.

2. You may need to use a strong motion from your cueing arm so that your dog understands that he should continue to take the last jump even though you are slowing down. Once he completes that jump, he should wrap tightly to come toward you.

Speed Change Issues

The biggest issue with the skill of changing speeds is forgetting to think about it at all. Most handlers give lots of attention to how they will handle individual obstacles, but many overlook the power of acceleration and deceleration. When you prepare to run an exercise in class or a complete course at a trial, pay significant attention to places where your dog can dig in and run and places where deceleration will prepare him to change direction. Acceleration will improve your course times by energizing your dog. Deceleration will improve your course times by tightening turns.

Mental Practice

Figure 5.5 is another sequence that includes sections where you will run like the wind and places where you will want to decelerate. Decide where you would change speeds and how you would cross.

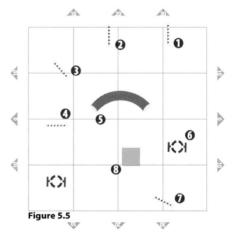

Answer: The handler should accelerate from obstacles #1 to #3. Before jump #4, the handler should decelerate because the dog needs to know there is a turn to the tunnel. The handler could front cross between jump #4 and the tunnel or rear cross the tunnel. (The front cross eliminates the danger of pulling the dog out of the tunnel on the cross. However, it needs to be executed closely to the tunnel to avoid pushing the dog toward the tire dummy jump.) The handler should accelerate through the tire and then decelerate before jump #7 to cue the pull to the table. It is the handler's choice whether to pull the dog to the table on the left hand or front cross and push the dog to the table.

Figure 5.5

Concluding Thoughts

It is useful to ask a friend to videotape you while you run a sequence that requires at least two speed changes. The difference in your body language between acceleration and deceleration should be easy to "read." Naturally, your very best feedback will come from your dog because he is the one who needs to understand and react to your communication.

6 Shoulder Pull

One of the primary differences between novice courses and intermediate courses is that they require teams to change direction more often. Your ability to turn your dog efficiently will make the difference between finishing intermediate runs and placing in the ribbons.

There are three main methods that we will discuss for switching directions on a course: the shoulder pull, the front cross (see Chapter 7), and the rear cross (see Chapter 8). We'll start with the shoulder pull, also called the post turn by some handlers, which is the most basic.

To execute a shoulder pull, the handler draws the dog around herself but doesn't switch sides. (See Photo 6.A.) You can see why the name "post turn" fits because the handler becomes a post around which the dog runs to change direction. The sequence in Figure 6.1 has two post turns. The first is a 90-degree turn from jump #3 to jump #4. Without clear handling, the dog could easily think that the tire is the correct obstacle. The second post turn is jump #6 to jump #7. This is a more challenging version because the dog must make a 180-degree turn.

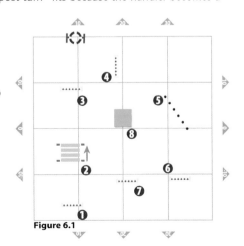

Figure 6.1

Prerequisite Skills

There are three things you need to know to help your dog make an efficient shoulder pull:

1. how to teach him to stay on the outside of a curve when running with you

6.A: To execute a shoulder pull, the handler draws the dog around herself but doesn't switch sides.

2. how to handle laterally

3. how to use your deceleration at the obstacle before the turn

By handling laterally, you allow your dog to see the second obstacle in the turn rather than blocking his view. (See Photo 6.B.) You also give him room to run a tight line from the first to the second obstacle. Your deceleration cues your dog that a change of direction is coming and prevents him from running straight ahead and missing the turn altogether. Figure 6.2 shows the correct and incorrect positions for executing this skill.

After you decelerate, you need to tell your dog what direction he will be going in after he lands. To communicate that he should come toward you, clearly rotate your shoulders and feet toward the second obstacle. Your rotation should precede your dog's jumping so that he knows where he is going when he lands. If your rotation is timely, your dog will begin turning his body in the air as you have been practicing, and he will land knowing exactly where he is going next.

Teaching the Shoulder Pull

As you teach this turn to your dog, it is useful to think of yourself as pulling him toward you. Imagine that you are magnetized and are drawing your dog tightly around yourself.

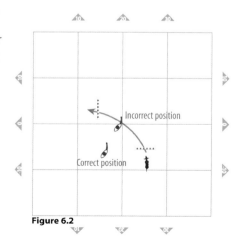

Incorrect position

Correct position

Figure 6.2

Intermediate Handling Skills

6.B: By handling laterally, you allow your dog to see the second obstacle in the turn.

Step 1

This is a simple review from your novice training to get your dog thinking about a directional change. Start with a single jump.

1. With your dog on your right, send him over the jump and move forward.
2. As soon as he commits to taking the jump, rotate your feet and shoulders 90 degrees to your left.
3. Reinforce your dog by tossing the toy or cookie forward so that he doesn't look at you excessively. The toss should come from the hand that is farthest from your dog.
4. Repeat on both sides.

Step 2

1. This time, rotate 180 degrees once your dog commits to jump. He should jump and then run around you to get the toy or cookie, as if you are a post.
2. Repeat on both sides.

Step 3

Now you are ready to bring another obstacle into play. Add one jump at a 90-degree angle to the first.

1. Maintaining your lateral distance, send your dog over the first jump.
2. Drive toward the jump with speed and then slow down a bit to cue the turn before he jumps. (See Photo 6.C.)
3. Once you know that he is committed to jumping, rotate toward the second jump. (See Photo 6.D.)
4. Drive past the second jump and toss a toy or cookie to reinforce him if he completes both obstacles. (See Photo 6.E.)
5. Repeat on both sides.

Shoulder Pull

Step 4

Once your dog can execute this right-angle turn easily going in both directions, you are ready to make this a bit more challenging by adding an obstacle straight ahead that might call your dog's name—use an obstacle that your dog particularly likes. (See Photo 6.F.)

1. Start with the new obstacle at a distance that is not too much of a draw.
2. Gradually move it closer until it becomes a serious discrimination. On Figure 6.3, I have added the table and moved it gradually closer to the turn as the dog understands the game.

Step 5

After your dog successfully completes the shoulder pull to the jump a few times with the table relatively close by, it is time to get him thinking.

1. Change the game and send him from the first jump to the table. Then return to pulling him around the corner to the second jump.
2. Alternate several times between using your shoulder pull to steer your dog around the corner from jump to jump and sending him straight forward from the first jump to the table. This will encourage your dog to pay attention to your cues rather than operate on autopilot.

Step 6

Next you will add some speed. Add any variety of obstacles to get your dog really going before you get to the turn. It is much easier for your dog to continue running straight ahead than to turn when he is running at full speed.

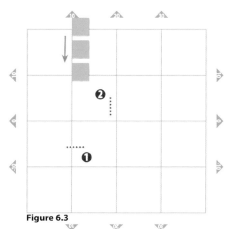

Figure 6.3

Step 7

At this level, make the shoulder pull more challenging by asking your dog to pull away from an easier obstacle toward a more difficult obstacle. In the sequence in Figure 6.4, the dog must turn to

Intermediate Handling Skills

6.C: Decelerate before your dog jumps to cue the turn.
6.D: Once you know that he is committed to jumping, rotate toward the second jump.
6.E: Drive past the second jump.
6.F: Challenge your dog by adding an obstacle straight ahead that he loves.

the right for the weaves and resist the urge to take the jump ahead.

At this skill level, handling correctly is immensely important. If the handler goes too far forward and the dog passes the poles, it will be very difficult for him to come back to get the correct entry. However, if the handler remains lateral, decelerates to cue the turn, and rotates smoothly once the dog is preparing to jump, the dog can find the weaves nicely. On Figure 6.4, I have indicated the correct and incorrect path for the post turn.

Shoulder Pull Issues

When executing a shoulder pull, the handler runs a shorter distance than her dog. This means that handlers often end up ahead of their dogs, even with adequate deceleration to cue the turn. Getting ahead of your dog is not a bad thing as long as you want him to keep driving forward.

6.G: Whenever you get ahead of your dog, look back over your shoulder and use your hand to indicate the next obstacle.

However, it is common for handlers to lose eye contact with their dog as they race forward—all the dog sees is his handler's back. This is a formula for the dog to either knock a bar or skip the jump because he wants to catch up with his handler. Whenever you get ahead of your dog, look back over your shoulder at him and use your hand to indicate the obstacle that you want him to take so that he knows it is important. (See Photo 6.G.)

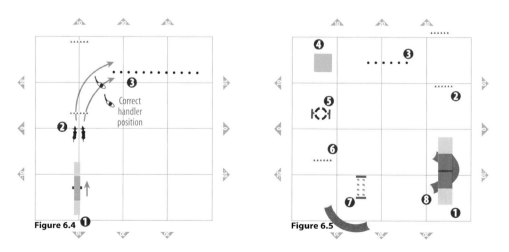

Figure 6.4

Correct handler position

Figure 6.5

Intermediate Handling Skills

Mental Practice

Here is a sequence for you to think about. There are two shoulder pulls in Figure 6.5. Identify those first. Assuming that your dog is comfortable with all of the obstacles, which one is likely to be more difficult? How will you handle each of them?

Answer: The first shoulder pull is between jump #2 and the short set of weaves. We have already discussed how to handle a turn from a jump to the weave poles. The second turn is jump #6 to the spread jump #7. This is liable to be the more challenging because of the tunnel straight ahead. If you push in past jump #6 or rotate too late, you are likely to watch your pup vanish into the tunnel. Remember to decelerate before jump #6 to cue your dog that he will be turning. Stay as lateral as your dog will allow without pulling him off the jump. Rotate smoothly toward jump #7 before he takes jump #6. If you don't tell him that he is turning until he lands, he will have locked onto the tunnel and it will be too late to call him off.

> ### Take Note
> If at any time your dog doesn't do what you think you are asking, check your own body language. For example, if your dog goes straight ahead over an obstacle rather than pulling around a corner, stop right where you are. You will likely see that your feet and shoulders are facing straight ahead rather than rotated to face the second obstacle.

Concluding Thoughts

At the novice level, you undoubtedly worked on the shoulder pull, perhaps without ever even knowing the name, and you were likely pleased if your dog came around the corner with you. Your job at the intermediate level is to refine your communication with your dog so that he knows exactly where he is going and corners so efficiently that you can shave time on course.

There are two additional types of post turns that are a bit more challenging. We will review the 180-degree turn and the 270-degree turn in Chapter 9.

7
Front Cross

I n this chapter, we will review the second tool at your disposal for changing directions on course: the front cross. When well executed, this maneuver is the most powerful tool for communicating a turn in agility. This statement might cause some late-night debate among hardcore competitors, but I think you will find that when you work to get ahead of your dog so that you can front cross to indicate the next obstacle, it leaves little doubt where you are headed.

Since my earlier book, *The Beginner's Guide to Dog Agility*, the technique for performing the front cross has been refined to allow the dog to run a much shorter line between two obstacles on a turn. My understanding of this high-tech front cross has been strongly influenced by Greg Derrett, a top-notch agility competitor in the United Kingdom who has created a system for handling that he describes in a series of DVDs. (The DVDs can be found at www.gtagility.com.)

A Brief Review

The front cross is one of two options when you need to change directions and switch your dog to the opposite hand. The other option is the rear cross. (See Chapter 8.) Figure 7.1 is a simple map that shows that the handler has crossed to switch her dog from the left hand to the right hand. The purpose of the cross is, of course, to keep the handler on the inside of the arc.

In Figure 7.1, we don't know if the handler has front crossed or rear crossed. In Figure 7.2, you can easily identify the front cross because the

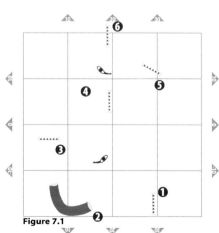

Figure 7.1

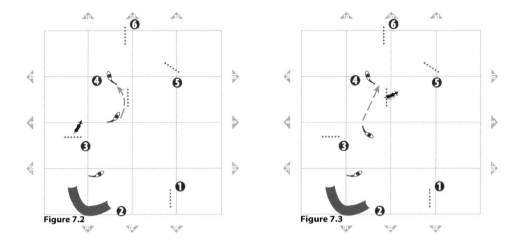

Figure 7.2

Figure 7.3

handler has moved ahead of the dog and rotated in front to pick him up on the opposite hand. In Figure 7.3, the rear cross, the handler has sent the dog ahead over the next obstacle, jump #4, and cut across his path to pick him up on the other hand.

Every time you encounter a change of direction on course that requires a change of hands, you will have to decide which type of cross will work better. There is no hard and fast rule, but you need to handle both with confidence to tackle intermediate courses. I occasionally see competitors who lock onto one type of cross and try to use it in every situation. This limits their skills dramatically on complex courses with multiple turns.

Prerequisite Skills

There are two key skills that you must know:
1. how to handle laterally
2. how to use your deceleration at the obstacle before the turn

My students sometimes tell me that they can't front cross because their dog is fast and gets ahead of them. The reality is that you can front cross with any dog if you take the time to teach

> **Take Note**
> The front cross should be used only when there is a change of direction on course. As long as you use it consistently in this way, your dog will understand that when you start to cross, he needs to prepare to switch directions. Occasionally, I see folks trying to front cross in the middle of a straight line of obstacles. This will confuse your dog and is a formula for a collision.

him to work laterally. If you watch the fastest teams in the world, you will see the handlers front crossing frequently. They are able to do this because they can move away from their dog, which gives them enough space to cross. If you must escort your pup to each obstacle, you simply don't have enough room to cross without running into each other. Make sure to teach your dog that he can carry away from you to complete the obstacle you are indicating before you work on this skill.

The High-Tech Front Cross

Learning to cross at a higher level may require a bit of unlearning—it sure has for me! Take a look at Figure 7.4, which indicates the handler's path on a front cross. You will note that the handler has run clear across the face of jump #3 to cross. This is the spot where most novices have learned to cross. Can you see the problem with the location of this cross?

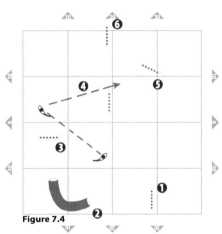

Figure 7.4

When the handler chooses this path, she has to run a long way to cross and then has to push the dog back to jump #4. Obviously, this takes a lot of time.

There is a second issue with the old system of front crossing. We began to front cross when the dog was in the air or even after he had landed. Kiss those days good-bye. With your new approach, you are going to start to cue your dog before he has even jumped. Here is how the new system works. (See Figure 7.5.) The handler sends the dog to jump #3, runs as closely as possible to the next jump, and front crosses as soon as the dog has committed to taking the jump. By the time the dog lands, the handler has already switched hands to tell him a change of direction is coming, has already rotated to pick up the dog on the right hand, and is driving past jump #4.

Given the location of this cross, there is no doubt in the dog's mind where he is headed. Imagine the savings in distance and time!

Teaching the Front Cross

Performing a great front cross has six recognizable steps you can master. Your challenge is not only to learn to put them into action but also to use them consistently in practice and at trials so that your

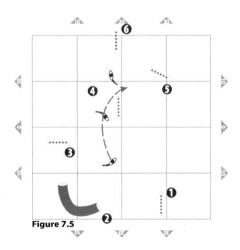

Figure 7.5

7.A: Step #1 of your intermediate front cross is to slow down enough so that your dog collects his stride.
7.B: Send him to the next obstacle while you stay off to the side.
7.C: Move toward the obstacle where you are going to cross, start your rotation, and switch hands.
7.D: As soon as you have completed your cross, start driving forward.

dog reads them clearly. This takes both repetition and discipline but will drastically elevate your handling skills. The key principles are:

Step 1: Decelerate
As you know, slowing down tells your dog a turn is coming. Step 1 of your intermediate front cross is to slow down enough so that your dog collects his stride in preparation for a direction change. (See Photo 7.A.)

Step 2: Send Your Dog to the Next Obstacle
As you practiced with lateral distance work, send your dog to the next obstacle while you stay off to the side. (See Photo 7.B.) In Figure 7.5, you are sending your dog to jump #3. Keep your arm at shoulder level to tell him that you want him to continue to travel forward.

Intermediate Handling Skills

Step 3: Move Toward the Next Obstacle

As soon as your dog commits to the next obstacle, slide toward the obstacle where you are going to cross. Using Figure 7.5, you would move toward the first stanchion of jump #4.

Step 4: Start Your Rotation Before Your Dog Jumps

Because your dog is focused on jump #3, you are free to start your rotation before he even jumps. Ideally, you should start your front cross at the first stanchion and finish your cross by the second stanchion of jump #4. This will leave a clear path open for your dog. (See Photo 7.C.)

Step 5: As You Rotate, Switch Arms

You have probably been switching from left arm to right arm or vice versa as part of your crosses already. The difference now is that you will start much earlier and complete the arm switch along with your rotation so that your dog lands already knowing which way you are going.

Step 6: Move Forward Dynamically

As soon as you have completed your cross, start driving forward. (See Photo 7.D.) There is a tendency to cross and then wait for the dog. If you have crossed in the correct spot, your dog will know right where you are headed, so there is no need to wait around.

You may want to practice crossing with as few steps as possible and moving forward as you rotate. I find that if I mince my steps, I have a tendency to twirl in place. When I can rotate in three or four steps, with each step carrying me forward, I am much less likely to stall out and waste time.

Putting Front Cross Principles Into Action

Let's look at two typical configurations where you might need to front cross. In the first example, Figure 7.6, the handler is decelerating and sending the dog out to jump #3. The second figure has moved toward jump #4 and started the cross by rotating and switching arms once the dog commits to jump #3. The third figure has completed the cross at the far stanchion and is already driving forward.

Let's take a look at a second example in Figure 7.7. Once again, the first figure is sending the dog out to jump #3. The second figure has slowed down, angled toward the next obstacle, and started the cross by rotating and switching arms just as the dog has committed to jump #3. The third figure has completed the cross at the far stanchion and is already driving forward. You can

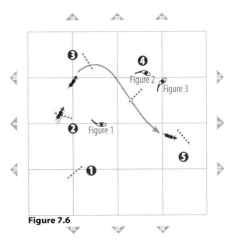

Figure 7.6

65

Front Cross

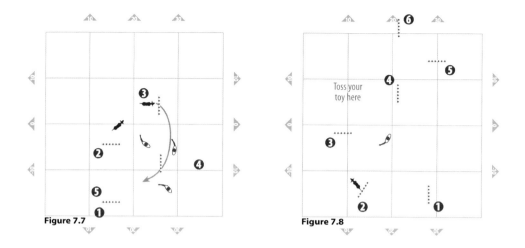

Figure 7.7

Figure 7.8

see how tight the dog's path should be between jumps #3 and #4. When I first started working this type of front cross, I worried that my dog couldn't jump at such a sharp angle. He could. I also felt as if I might run into the jump, but if I kept moving forward from stanchion to stanchion in my rotation, I cleared it handily.

Handling a Front Cross Sequence: Jumps

Set up a sequence as set forth in Figure 7.8. If you have only three jumps, you can do the exercise by setting them up to match obstacles #1 to #3.

Step 1

To get started, do a few practices to remind your dog that you like it when he travels to an obstacle while you maintain a lateral distance.

1. Start with your toy or food bag in your right hand. Send your dog over jumps #1 and #2.
2. Remain to the side while you direct your dog over jump #3. Toss his toy where indicated on Figure 7.8 to reward his forward focus.

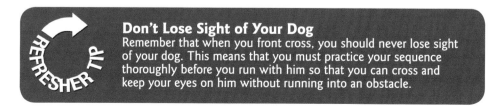

Don't Lose Sight of Your Dog
Remember that when you front cross, you should never lose sight of your dog. This means that you must practice your sequence thoroughly before you run with him so that you can cross and keep your eyes on him without running into an obstacle.

The biggest challenge in executing a timely front cross is understanding when your dog is committed to taking an obstacle.

Step 2
Now we will add your cross and reinforce your dog for coming in to your right hand.
1. Send your dog over the first three jumps.
2. Cross as close to jump #4 as possible. Give your pup a small cookie out of your right hand.
3. Repeat several times.

Step 3
At this level, you will reward your dog for taking jump #4 after reading your front cross.
1. Send your dog over the first three jumps, cross, and drive past the jump.
2. Toss the toy after your dog takes the fourth jump.

Step 4
Complete the rest of the sequence by using your shoulder pull to show your dog jumps #5 and #6.

Step 5
Set up the mirror image of this sequence and practice crossing in the other direction. Periodically reinforce your dog at jump #3 for letting you keep your lateral distance.

Step 6
Set up the other sequences in this chapter, and practice putting the front-cross principles into action.

Front Cross

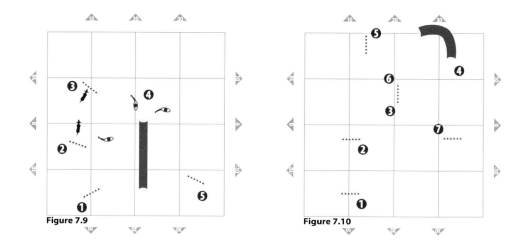

Figure 7.9

Figure 7.10

Handling a Front Cross Sequence: Other Obstacles

Not all front crosses happen at jumps, of course, but the principles are the same. Figure 7.9 features an example of a cross to the tunnel. The cross is necessary to get you in position for the jump that follows the contact. Note the tight path that the handler travels to get to the tunnel. The strategy would be exactly the same if the tunnel were any other obstacle, including the contact equipment.

You might look at this and ask why you wouldn't just rear cross the tunnel. The answer is that you could, but the cross would slice across the tunnel in a way that has a high probability of pulling the dog out.

Front Cross Issues

The biggest challenge in executing a timely front cross is understanding when your dog is committed to taking an obstacle. Intellectually, we understand that we should begin to cross when the dog is committed to the obstacle that precedes the front cross. However, once we are on course, we read commitment as the moment when our dog's nose is right at the obstacle. When we start our rotation at this moment, we are crossing while our dog is in the air, which results in a knocked bar or wide turn. In reality, dogs commit to an obstacle many strides before they get there. Once you learn to read this commitment, it will free you up to front cross early enough to tell your dog clearly where he is going.

Plan a session with an agility friend. Set up three jumps in a pattern that encourages a front cross. For example, see jumps #2 to #4 in Figure 7.8. Call your dog over the first two jumps and then front cross to send him over the third while your friend watches. Ask her to comment about the location of your dog when you initiated the cross. Push the envelope and cross earlier than you ever have before.

Intermediate Handling Skills

Once you learn to read your dog's commitment to an obstacle, you will be freed up to front cross earlier.

Mental Practice

Most intermediate courses have more than one front cross, as you will find in Figure 7.10. Here is a sequence that offers two opportunities to practice. Although you could rear cross the tunnel, stick to your front cross for now.

Answer: Did you find your two front crosses? They are between jumps #2 and #3 and between jumps #5 and #6. Check that you applied each of the six principles as you visualized yourself handling this sequence.

Concluding Thoughts

With just a few jumps, you can practice front-cross skills until your timing is clear and consistent. If you have a friend who can videotape you, this is a wonderful opportunity to see if you are putting the principles into action. Once you have confidence in your ability to front cross, you will find many places on course to put this strategy into action.

8
Rear Cross

In this chapter, we will review the third tool at your disposal for changing directions on course: the rear cross. In *The Beginner's Guide to Dog Agility*, I reviewed the basics of the rear cross, but like the front cross, handling of the rear cross has evolved to become more precise since then.

As I mentioned in the last chapter, I think highly of Greg Derrett's system of handling and have incorporated his thoughts about the rear cross. What I have learned from him and hope to teach you is that it is essential to develop a handling system in which you cue your dog the same way every time you encounter the same type of challenge. In this case, we will consider the exact cues you will use every time you rear cross.

A Brief Review

As you remember, to execute the rear cross, the handler sends the dog forward to perform an obstacle such as

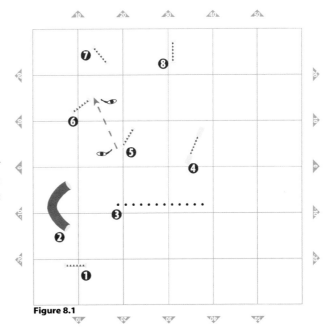

Figure 8.1

a jump or tunnel and then crosses the dog's path from behind. (See Photo 8.A.) As soon as the handler switches sides, she accelerates to pick up the dog on the opposite hand.

Handlers choose the rear cross to change directions on course rather than the front cross for three reasons: 1.) if you simply can't get enough lateral distance to get in a front cross; 2.) if there is an off-course obstacle straight ahead and you think that you might cue that obstacle instead of the correct obstacle by moving too far forward; 3.) if the course configuration makes it the only reasonable option.

Figure 8.1 is a sequence from a trial in which a rear cross was the only reasonable option. The wings on jump #4 made it impossible to

8.A: To execute the rear cross, the handler crosses the dog's path from behind.

front cross between the weave poles and that jump. The handler had to get to the inside on the pinwheel formed by jumps #6 to #8.

Prerequisite Skills

There are two skills that are required to rear cross smoothly:
1. Your dog must be willing to run ahead of you on cue.
2. You must use acceleration after you cross.

If your dog runs at your side, there is simply no room for you to switch sides behind him. You will be limited to front crossing in situations where you need to switch sides, and this can be awkward. Take some time to teach your dog that it is okay to run on and take the next obstacle.

Teaching the Rear Cross

In the past, we tried three strategies to alert the dog that we were going to rear cross, none of which worked to create the kind of consistency we wanted. Many of us adopted a motion in which we flicked our hand toward the obstacle where we wanted the dog to run after the cross.

Intermediate Handling Skills

This motion resembled the letter "c" drawn from the bottom up. On the course map in Figure 8.1, the handler would have flicked her right hand using this motion toward jump #7. The problem was that many dogs started to anticipate a rear cross any time the handler raised her arm and flipped away in the wrong direction, even when the course went straight ahead. Then we tried shaping the rear cross by first pulling the dog toward us and then pushing him into the turn with our outside arm. This confused the dog about whether the handler was rear crossing or executing a post turn. Last, we tried switching to our outside arm to cue the cross, but dogs read the arm change, as they should have, as a front cross.

It became clear that we needed a cue for the rear cross that couldn't be confused with another cue and provided clear information about what was coming. The answer was to use our bodies rather than our arms as the primary communication tool.

The newer method of rear crossing is relatively simple, but it may take a bit of retraining for you if you have been practicing with one of the older methods. Once again, I speak from personal experience. I still ask my teacher to watch me regularly as I rear cross to make sure that I don't pull away from my dog rather than moving toward my dog.

Once you have identified a place on course where a rear cross is your best choice, there are five steps to executing this strategy:

Step 1: Find the Diagonal

Before you run, find the diagonal between the two obstacles where you plan to cross. Figure 8.2 shows an example.

Step 2: Push Into Your Dog on the Diagonal Line

As your dog clears the obstacle before the cross, run on that diagonal line pushing toward him, as

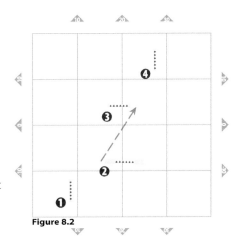

Figure 8.2

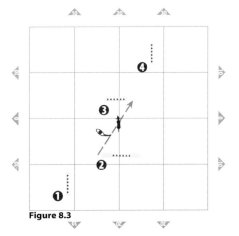

Figure 8.3

73

Rear Cross

8.B: As your dog clears the obstacle before the cross, run on the diagonal line, pushing toward him.

8.C: As he drives ahead and commits to the jump, cross behind him on the same diagonal line.

8.D: As soon as you cross, speed up and drive toward the correct obstacle.

pictured in Figure 8.3. (See Photo 8.B.) This will tell him that something is up. (Later we will discuss how you can teach your dog to take the jump or other obstacle even though you are pushing into his space.)

Step 3: Cross Your Dog's Path
As your dog drives ahead and commits to the jumps, cross behind him on the same diagonal line, as pictured in Figure 8.4. (See Photo 8.C.) This will put you in the position to pick him up on the opposite hand as he lands. As soon as he sees you appear on the "new" side, he will know that you are changing directions.

Step 4: Accelerate to Pick Him Up on the New Hand
As soon as you cross, speed up and drive toward the correct obstacle. (See Photo 8.D.) This will keep your dog from spinning in the wrong direction in many cases, and he will land knowing exactly where you are going. That is the sign of a good system.

Step 5: Use Your Arms Consistently
Some trainers recommend using no arms at all during this move, simply running hard on the diagonal, to prevent any confusion on the dog's part with an arm change. Other trainers use a small forward cue with the arm closest to the dog to tell him to drive forward at the same time they move diagonally. As soon as they cross behind, they switch cueing hands to use the hand closest to

Intermediate Handling Skills

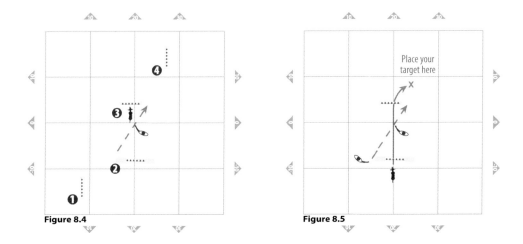

Figure 8.4

Figure 8.5

Place your target here

the dog. See what works best for your dog, but be careful that you do the same thing every time once you decide. Don't fall into the habit of using elaborate arm motions.

Handling a Rear Cross Sequence

Naturally, you must teach your dog what it means when you run toward him lest you push him around the obstacle where he is headed. Herding breeds can be particularly uncomfortable with your moving into their personal bubble, much like you feel when someone stands too closely to you. In these exercises, start with your dog rather than leading out because you want to give him room to drive ahead of you.

Remember that your dog should never spin in the incorrect direction when he lands. This eats up a lot of time and stops your forward momentum.

Step 1

1. Set up two parallel jumps and identify the diagonal line you plan to run.
2. Place a target out beyond the second jump to give your dog something to think about other than your movement. (See Photo 8.E.) This can be a toy, cookie bag, or food-stuffed plastic bottle. Placement of the target should be offset slightly so that your dog has to make a small turn toward the new direction but not so wide that he just skips the second jump to get it. (See Figure 8.5.)
3. Send your dog over the first jump and run your diagonal line.
4. As soon as he is committed to the second jump, cross behind him and switch hands. Race out and play, or deliver another cookie.
5. Repeat this just a few times until your dog understands that he should take the obstacle despite your movement. Practice with him on both sides.

8.E: Place a target out beyond the second jump to give your dog something to think about other than your movement.
8.F: At Step #2, carry the toy or cookie in your hand that's farthest away from your dog.
8.G: Toss as closely as possible to the spot you were placing the target before.
8.H: It is time to add the third obstacle toward which your dog is turning.

Step 2

1. When your dog is driving ahead nicely while you cross, change the delivery of the reinforcement. Rather than placing it onto the ground, toss the toy or cookie after your dog commits to jumping. Start by carrying your toy or cookie in your hand farthest away from the dog. (See Photo 8.F.) After you cross, this will be the hand closest to your dog. Toss as closely as possible to the spot you were placing the target before. (See Photo 8.G.)

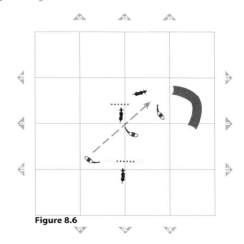

Figure 8.6

Intermediate Handling Skills

2. If you find running the diagonal line and tossing difficult, ask your training buddy to stand to the side and deliver the reward after your dog jumps.
3. As before, practice with your dog on both sides so that he doesn't get "one sided."

Step 3

Once your dog accepts your cross without a spin in the wrong direction, it is time to add the third obstacle toward which he is turning. (See Photo 8.H.) This can be a jump or a tunnel. To warm up your dog, repeat Step 2, tossing your toy closer to the third obstacle each time. If he takes the jump or tunnel, great, but you are not trying for that. You are just showing him the turn. Now you are ready to do all three obstacles. (See Figure 8.6.)

1. Give your dog his command to jump, and run your diagonal between the first two jumps.
2. Pick up your dog on your left hand and continue to accelerate forward while giving him the command for the third obstacle.
3. If the maneuver goes smoothly, reward your dog by tossing his toy or cookie onto the landing side of the third obstacle after he clears the jump or as he exits the tunnel.
4. Move the third obstacle to the other side so that you are running the diagonal in the opposite direction. Your dog will be turning to his left.

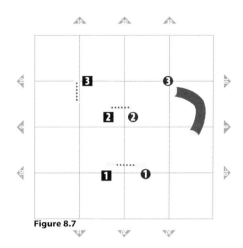
Figure 8.7

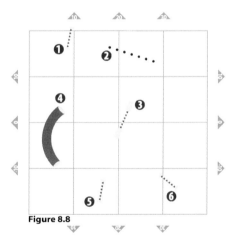
Figure 8.8

Practicing the Rear Cross

As your dog gains experience with the rear cross, you can practice rear crossing most obstacles. However, there are two places that require caution. Rear crossing the teeter is not recommended for intermediate dogs because the move might pull them off the side. Also, consider carefully whether to rear cross at a triple or a double jump. Dogs often knock bars on the spread jumps if the handler moves across.

Step 4
Add a fourth obstacle, as pictured in Figure 8.7. Alternate rear crossing to jump #3 (start with the dog on your left) and to the tunnel (start with the dog on your right).

Step 5
It is time to practice your rear crossing skill on a different obstacle. On the sequence pictured in Figure 8.8, start with your dog on your left and practice a rear cross at the tunnel, and then drive to jumps #5 and #6. As you approach the tunnel, run diagonally to cue your dog.

You may need to execute a rear cross to any obstacle, including the contacts, when you get to the excellent level. Be cautious about rear crossing on those until your dog is very experienced because it is easy to pull him off and give him a scare.

Rear Cross Issues
If your dog spins after he jumps rather than turning in the direction of the obstacle you are cueing, there is one of three problems: 1.) First, he may never have become comfortable with losing sight of you as you cross behind him. He spins around because that's where he saw you last. If this is the case, you need to play a game in which you put your dog in a *sit-stay* and move back and forth across his tail while he faces away from you. He should turn his head in both directions to find you without getting up. Click and treat each time he turns his head back to find you. 2.) Second, you may be crossing too slowly so that he doesn't get the information in time to turn in the correct direction. Your dog should know before he starts to jump that he is going to turn because he sees that you have switched sides. To accomplish this, move diagonally toward him more assertively and cross as soon as you can. 3.) Third, some handlers cross and then stop moving forward. As your dog lands, accelerate and drive forward toward the obstacle following the cross.

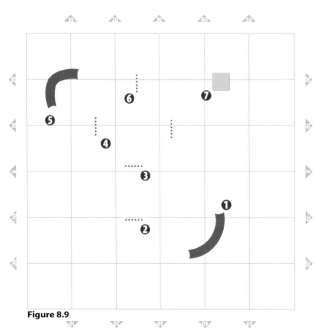

Figure 8.9

Mental Practice
Take a look at Figure 8.9 and decide where you would rear cross. Where would you place your rear cross diagonal?

Answer: There are two good places to rear cross in this

Intermediate Handling Skills

If you practice the system described in this chapter, you will handle rear crosses confidently and smoothly.

sequence. Clearly, you need to cross to pull your dog toward jump #4. Your diagonal cue would be run between jumps #2 and #3. Then there is another rear cross at the #5 tunnel. Run diagonally between the #4 jump and the tunnel, but be careful not to angle so much that you block the tunnel entry.

Concluding Thoughts

When you are running intermediate courses, you must cross frequently and will often need to choose between rear and front crosses. In general, well-executed front crosses are more efficient because you are in front of your dog and steering his head. My classes often tease me that we spend three times as much time on front crossing than on rear crossing. I plead guilty. However, there simply are times that the rear cross is the only option because your dog is ahead of you or the configuration of obstacles won't let you get in position to front cross. If you practice the system described in this chapter, you will handle rear crosses confidently and smoothly.

9

180- and 270-Degree Turns

n this chapter, we will look at two turns that are named by the number of degrees of the angle. One requires the dog to make a 180-degree turn, and as you can guess, the other requires the dog to pull around a 270-degree corner. Historically, beginner-level agility courses had relatively gentle turns. These days, it is not uncommon to encounter 180-degree turns in beginner-level courses. At the intermediate level, it is guaranteed that you will frequently encounter both types of wide turns described in this chapter.

Figure 9.1 shows the 180-degree turn. Your goal is to handle your dog so that he completes this turn while staying as close to the jumps as possible to save time.

The 270-degree turn is a relative newcomer to agility. Until its introduction, agility competitors agonized over the 180-degree turn, which now seems like a leisurely drive in the park. Figure 9.2 shows what the 270 looks like.

These two turns are more challenging than what you have been doing because the dog doesn't actually see the obstacle that is coming after the turn. He is completely dependent on your body language to show him the path that he must run.

We will start by teaching your dog the 180-degree turn, which then leads to the 270. Have your toy handy so that you can reward your dog on the correct path exactly as you did when working on lateral distance in Chapter 4.

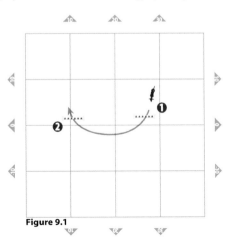

Figure 9.1

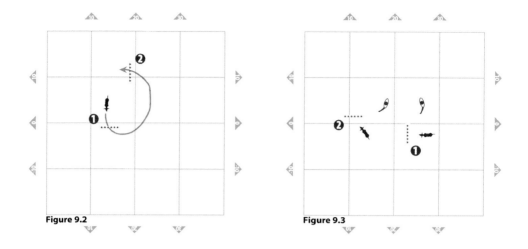

Figure 9.2   **Figure 9.3**

Prerequisite Skills

Both of these configurations are actually shoulder pulls with which you are familiar. That is, you change directions but your dog remains on the same hand. If he is able to handle a 90-degree shoulder pull, you are ready to get started with these new configurations.

Teaching the 180-Degree Turn

Teaching your dog to make this turn without ducking between the two jumps and missing the second jump is not hard if approached sequentially. I am going to suggest that you use your clicker during these lessons, although you may choose to use your marker word. You want to communicate clearly with your dog that you like it when he looks for and takes the second jump.

Step 1

This step is a simple review. As pictured in Figure 9.3, place two jumps at 90 degrees to each other approximately 6 feet (2 m) apart. Start with jumps set very low, about 2 inches (5 cm) for small dogs and 12 inches (30.5 cm) for large dogs.

1. With your dog on your left, send him over the first and then the second jump.
2. Click while he's between the uprights of the second jump.
3. Toss your toy or a food reward onto

9.A: Move in a path that keeps your shoulder directly across from your dog's shoulder.

Intermediate Handling Skills

9.B and 9.C: In small increments, rotate the first jump until the turn is up to 180 degrees.

the ground several feet (m) beyond his landing spot to help him drive on forward.

Move in a path that keeps your shoulder directly across from your dog's shoulder. (See Photo 9.A.) It is helpful to imagine that there is a wire from your shoulder to your dog's shoulder to help yourself stay in the correct position. Getting ahead of the dog is a common handling error, and doing so may cause him to duck behind you. Getting behind him is likely to cause him to dart in front of you.

Although the clicker provides the best feedback for dogs, it can sometimes cause them to knock bars. If you notice this, delay your click until your dog has cleared the bar. A short delay has an added benefit of keeping you from clicking accidentally when a bar comes down.

Step 2

In small increments, rotate the first jump until the turn is up to 180 degrees. (See Figure 9.4 and Photos 9.B and 9.C.) It is better to move the first rather than the second jump because then the dog knows where to find it as it becomes less visible. The distance between the jumps may vary depending on the size of your dog. Experiment with a distance that is comfortable for him.

In the beginning of teaching your dog this skill, you will likely need to move into the gap between the jumps to help him understand that he needs to stay outside the second jump. Continue to run in an arc that parallels your dog's path, and remember to line up your shoulder position with your dog's. (See Figure 9.5.)

There is some variety in the use of the arm to cue this turn. Traditionally, handlers extended their arm at shoulder height from jump to jump to communicate that the dog should stay out of the backside of the second obstacle. More recently, some handlers are experimenting with a quick flick of their hand to cue the dog to make the 180-degree turn. Pick an arm motion that is comfortable for you to use, and simply use it consistently so that your dog knows what you want.

Continue to mark the second jump with your clicker or marker word, and reinforce with a toy toss. This is hard work for dogs initially, so keep the game fun and rewarding. Make sure to practice this game going in both directions. Gradually raise the bars to your dog's full jump height.

180- and 270-Degree Turns

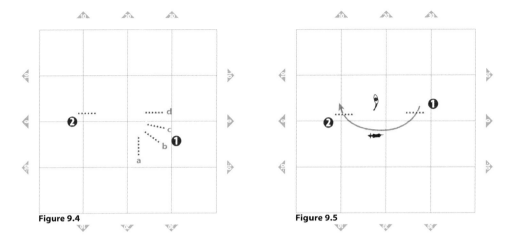

Figure 9.4

Figure 9.5

Step 3

As your dog understands his job on the 180, you will not need to travel as far into the zone between jumps as before. This will allow you to get positioned correctly for whatever the next obstacle might be. It will also encourage your dog to travel a shorter path between the jumps. As you gradually migrate farther away from the turn, continue to run a parallel path and stay across from your dog's shoulder. (See Figure 9.6.)

If at any time your dog starts to duck between jumps, there are two ways to help him. You can go farther into the gap for a repetition or two just to remind him what you want, or you can bring his toy out. Send him over jump #1 and then toss his toy onto the path you want him to run so that he finds the second obstacle. (See Figure 9.7.) This will serve to remind him that staying out away from you is rewarding. Toss from the hand that's farthest from your dog—holding it on the side closest to him may actually encourage him to come toward you rather than staying away. After a couple of tosses on the take-off side of the second jump, send him over the second jump and reinforce on the landing side by tossing his toy.

Some dogs, notably herding breeds, will get so excited about the toy that they skirt around the far side of the second jump. If you have this type of dog, don't accidentally toss the toy too early and reinforce him. Rather, if he skips the second jump, just say "Uh oh" and swing him around to the first jump to start over. As soon as he takes the second jump, mark it and toss the toy. I had to do this a number of times with my young Border Collie until she realized that there was no toy until she jumped.

> **Take Note**
> There is no need to jump your dog at full height all the time. In fact, you may prolong his career if you let him jump one height lower part of the time. It is even okay to mix jump heights on a training sequence so that he gets used to a variety of "looks."

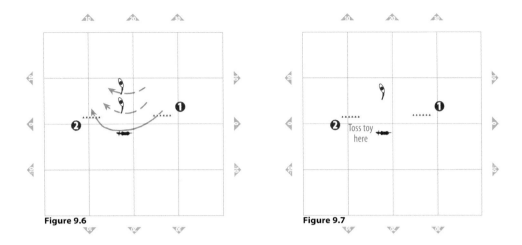

Figure 9.6

Figure 9.7

Step 4
Once your dog is experienced, vary the width of the 180 so that he is comfortable with a variety of "looks." In general, the wider the 180, the more difficult it is because the dog must hold out away from you over a longer distance. Make sure to practice each variation going in both directions.

Teaching the 270-Degree Turn
Once your dog consistently reads and handles the 180, you can increase the challenge to a 270-degree turn. The process will sound very familiar. Initially lower the jumps again so that your dog can concentrate on understanding what you want rather than on clearing bars.

Step 1
In tiny increments, move the first jump from 180 to 270 degrees. (See Photos 9.D and 9.E.) In following this process, your dog will become patterned to look for the second jump, which becomes less and less visible.

Once he commits to taking the first jump, start your rotation. As you did originally with the 180, you will likely need to move into the gap between the jumps to help him understand that he needs to stay outside of them. (See Photo 9.F.) Elevate your arm to cue your dog to stay out on the curve. Run parallel to the path that he needs to travel. Click when your dog is between the stanchions of jump #2, and throw his toy or food reward onto his path of travel, several feet (m) beyond his landing spot. (See Figure 9.9 and Photo 9.G.)

If at any point your dog becomes confused and starts ducking between the jumps, decrease the angle again. Be careful about too many repetitions of this exercise in one lesson because dogs can easily get tired of the concentration and control required. For any exercise, three to four repetitions in one training session is enough.

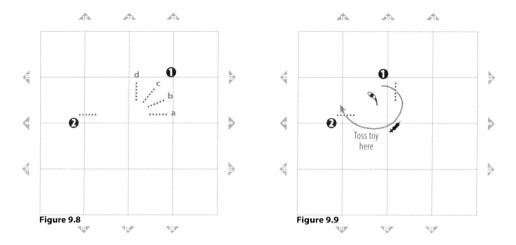

Figure 9.8   Figure 9.9

Step 2

When your dog stays out on the arc through the 270, it is time to migrate away, as shown in Figure 9.10. This will allow you to get to a good position for the obstacle that follows the turn. As you stay farther away, remember to keep your shoulder across from your dog's shoulder and your arm raised off to the side so that he understands that you want him to stay out on the arc. (See Photo 9.H.)

If at any time your dog starts to duck between jumps, bring your toy out. Use the same strategy you did with the 180, and toss your toy between the two jumps onto the path you want him to run.

Step 3

Once your dog is comfortable working the 270-degree angle with a low jump while you maintain good lateral distance, gradually increase the space between the two jumps while keeping them at a 270-degree angle. The wider the 270, the greater the challenge because the dog must hold the arc for a longer distance. This is particularly true with small dogs, who must take a great number of strides around big turns.

Step 4

Gradually raise the height of the jumps. Progress in 2-inch (5-cm) increments if possible. When you observe that your dog is completely comfortable at a given height, it is time to raise the bar to the

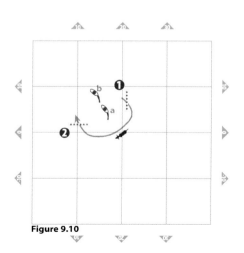

Figure 9.10

Intermediate Handling Skills

9.D

9.E

9.F

9.G

9.D and 9.E: In tiny increments, move the first jump from 180 to 270 degrees.
9.F: Move into the gap between the two jumps.
9.G: Throw your dog's toy or food reward on his path of travel.
9.H: As you stay farther away, remember to keep your shoulder across from your dog's shoulder.

9.H

next level and see how he does. If at any time you find him repeatedly sliding past jump #2 or looking uncomfortable trying to clear it, lower the jump. He is telling you that the bar is too high and he is not able to handle the height relative to his proximity to the jump. Lower the bar and again raise it very gradually to his official jump height.

Step 5

Once you have completed this process with your dog on your right, go back to Step 1 with him working on your left. The steps are likely to go faster than before.

180- and 270-Degree Turns

Sequences With Wide Turns

Once your dog can handle these turns in isolation, it is time to add additional obstacles. Start by adding just one obstacle before the turn, either the 180 or 270. This will keep your dog from approaching the turn with too much speed. Reinforce him if he completes the turn successfully without knocking the bar. Add one more obstacle at each training session so that your pup gradually builds his speed going into the turn. As your canine partner approaches these turns at speed, clearly decelerate before the first jump to cue him that he will need to collect to change directions. If you race too far forward, he will turn inefficiently or even take a more obvious obstacle that is straight ahead.

180 and 270 Issues

Most dogs understand the 180 turn fairly quickly, as long as the handler provides support around the arc with her arm and correct body position. However, the 270 turn is another matter. I often see dogs who start around the curve and then give up and cut between the two jumps. Sometimes this is because the handler has moved too far ahead of the dog, rather than staying across from his shoulder to provide support. The dog feels left behind, so he pulls in between jumps to catch up. Other times, the dog doesn't appear to understand his job. This is a simple training issue. Every time you go out to work on this turn, send your dog over the first jump and then toss his toy onto his path between the first and second jump. Repeat two or three times. This will teach him that you like it when he stays out on the arc. Don't ask for the second jump. Once you can tell that he is on the correct path to make the wide turn, cue him to take the second jump. If he gets it right, throw a party.

Mental Practice

Figure 9.11 includes both a 180- and a 270-degree turn. Identify the 180 turn. Where is the 270 turn? And for your bonus question, where is there a distinct possibility for the dog to go off course if the handler's attention wanders?

Answer: If you said that the 180 is formed by jumps #3 and #4, a gold star for you. If you found the 270 at jumps #6 to #7, another click and treat. Give yourself bonus points if you said that the potential off course is posed by tunnel #5. As the dog rounds the corner, it would be much easier for him to race forward into the tunnel than make the hard turn to the second jump (jump #4).

Body Language Versus Verbal Commands
Verbal commands are much less important in agility than in other dog sports. Things just happen too fast. If it is not language that steers the dog, what does? The answer is the handler's body movement and position relative to the obstacles and dog. The more sophisticated the handling maneuvers, the more precise you must be. This is highlighted by the precise handling required to master the 180- and 270-degree turns.

Intermediate Handling Skills

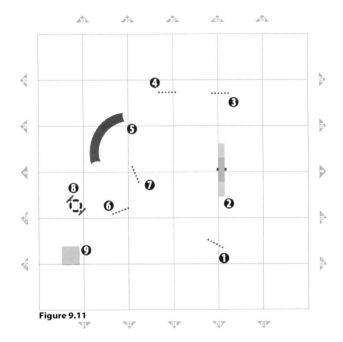

Figure 9.11

This is a place where the handler needs to make sure to rotate her shoulders quickly toward jump #7. If your dog loves tunnels, a vehement "Come!" might also be in order.

Concluding Thoughts

We often think about the self-control we want from our dogs, but the 180 and 270 are two intermediate skills that require considerable self-control from the handler. As your dog rounds these wide turns, he is traveling much farther than you. To maintain your position across from him, you need to decelerate dramatically—and this is true even with blistering-fast dogs. I often feel that I could have a snack while handling these turns. A friend suggested that I relax by thinking of myself as a great hostess who is escorting a guest into a party. No fuss, no hurry. This image helped me stop bolting ahead, which was causing my dog to miss the second obstacle in the turn. Once your dog locks in on the second obstacle, you can turn back into a high-powered competitor and take off running.

180- and 270-Degree Turns

10 Driving the Line

Novice courses are designed to test your dog's basic mastery of the individual obstacles. On intermediate-level courses, you will quickly encounter obstacle discriminations in which two obstacles are positioned very close together and you must help your dog select and perform the "correct" one.

Take a look at the sequence in Figure 10.1. There are two discriminations: First, the dog must choose to take the A-frame over the tunnel, and second, he must choose to take the tunnel rather than the A-frame. Discriminations can be created by the positioning of any of the agility obstacles.

When handling discriminations, you will put several skills that you have already learned to the test. Lateral distance, speed changes, and all three types of turns can be used to help dogs make a decision about where they should go. However, there are two additional specific skills that you will want to know to handle intermediate discriminations. In this chapter, we will discuss a skill called driving the line. In Chapter 11, we will focus on a second skill often called the false turn. In Chapter 12, we will pull it all together on a variety of discriminations.

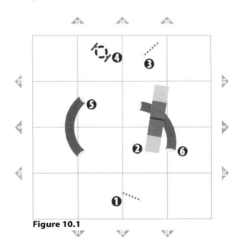

Figure 10.1

"Driving the Line" Versus "Pushing"

In past years, the handling strategy we are going to discuss in this chapter was generally called a "push." The name was well earned because handlers used their body language to "push" on the

Driving the line helps a dog choose the correct obstacle in a sequence.

dog's path to show him the correct obstacle. Dogs are just like people in the sense that they move away from us if we get too close.

More recently, the term "driving the line" has become popular to describe this maneuver. Emphasis has changed from pushing into the dog's space to teaching him to run parallel to the handler until he is given instructions about what to do next. On the sequence in Figure 10.1, the handler thinks about driving a straight line from tunnel to tunnel rather than working to push the dog off to the side until he finds the second tunnel.

In reality, I think that the two concepts combine perfectly. In Figure 10.1, it works very effectively if the handler drives directly from tunnel to tunnel with the dog on the right. Just as the dog passes the A-frame, she pushes toward his path with her closest hand to emphasize to him that he should take the outer obstacle.

Prerequisite Skills

There is one specific concept a dog must understand to drive the line. He must stay on the hand you are using to cue rather than ducking behind or in front of you. On the sequence in Figure 10.2, the handler picks up the dog out of tunnel #5 on her right hand and drives the line between the two tunnels with him on the right until he enters tunnel #6.

Although this may seem obvious, it is not uncommon for dogs to cross in front of or behind

Intermediate Handling Skills

their handler on this type of sequence to get to the A-frame. If your dog should make this mistake, go back to running circles with him as described in *The Beginner's Guide to Dog Agility*. Emphasize that he should always stay on the outside of the circle, and stop moving immediately if he moves in front of or behind you.

Teaching Your Dog to Drive the Line

To teach your dog to drive the line, we will start with a relatively easy discrimination and gradually increase the challenge. Discriminations are made harder depending on the attractiveness of the obstacle that the dog must pass. The sequence presented at the beginning of this chapter is quite tough because the dog must pass by the A-frame, and most dogs love this obstacle because they have been rewarded on it frequently.

Step 1

To begin, your dog will simply need to stay on your right hand and run from the tunnel to the jump, bypassing the table. This exercise will teach him that he should run past obstacles unless you specifically cue him to take them.

1. To handle the sequence shown in Figure 10.3, pick up your dog when he exits the tunnel.
2. Position yourself across from his head and run hard in a straight line toward jump #3. You have the greatest chance of influencing your dog's path when you "push" on his head.

Once you have successfully negotiated the three numbered obstacles, it is time to get your dog thinking. Change the exercise by directing him to the table for the third obstacle rather than going out to the jump. You will need to front cross or use a shoulder pull. End the exercise on the table a couple of times and then return to having your dog take jump #3. By alternating obstacles, you are teaching him to watch your body language carefully.

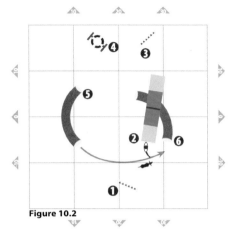

Figure 10.2

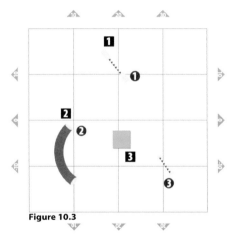

Figure 10.3

Take Note

Dogs are aware of what you are looking at—it's amazing but true. When you are driving the line, look at the obstacle you want. Try very hard not to glance at the incorrect obstacle.

Step 2

Next you will work on a discrimination, pictured in Figure 10.4, that is a bit harder. Most dogs love the tunnel, and it takes a good bit of self-control to run past an obvious entry.

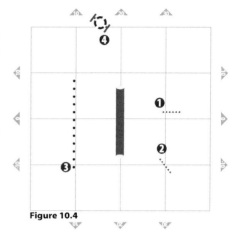

Figure 10.4

1. With your dog on your left hand, cue him to take jumps #2 and #3. Immediately drive the line directly to the weaves. (This exercise is not about finding the correct weave pole entry, so you may want to put on your guides to help your dog be successful.)

2. After a couple of successful runs, switch gears and ask your dog to take the tunnel. You will again draw on your front cross or shoulder pull between jump #2 and the tunnel to help your dog find the tunnel.

3. Then return to taking the weaves as the third obstacle. Since he is now hyper-aware of the tunnel, drive the line strongly between the jump and weaves.

Step 3

Next we will add a contact obstacle, as shown in Figure 10.5. Remember that the juxtaposition of tunnel and A-frame or dogwalk creates the most challenging configurations for driving the line. (You may need a new tool, called a gate. It is a barrier that you can use to keep your dog from making a mistake while he is learning. It is easy to assemble one with plastic pipe and a bit of plastic netting. You can find the parts at any store that sells irrigation supplies and at many online PVC retailers.)

Pull a tunnel under the A-frame as demonstrated in Figure 10.5. Then place your gate across the A-frame. This will show your dog that you don't want him to perform that obstacle at this time.

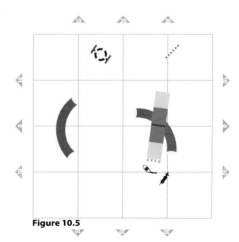

Figure 10.5

1. Start with your dog quite close to the tunnel and on your left hand.

2. When he glances at the tunnel, release him and send him in. (See Photo 10.A.) Make sure not to veer off before he disappears in the tunnel, or you will cause him to reverse course and take the A-frame.

3. Gradually move your dog back farther and farther so that you are driving him past the base of the A-frame. (See Photo 10.B.) This requires him to read your body language and

Intermediate Handling Skills

make an active choice about which obstacle to take. If your dog is interested in the A-frame, continue to use your gate across the contact.

You can help your dog by changing the way you use your arm and hand at this level. Rather than drawing the path for him as you generally do, push your hand strongly toward his path, as the arrow on Figure 10.6 indicates. This powerful motion tells your dog where you want him to run so that he will simply run toward the correct obstacle.

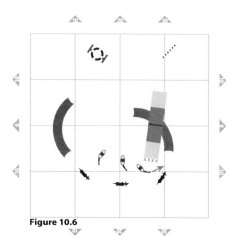

Figure 10.6

10.A

10.B

10.C

10.D

10.A: When your dog glances at the tunnel, release him and send him in.
10.B: Gradually move back farther so that you are driving him past the base of the A-frame.
10.C: Add another obstacle before the discrimination.
10.D: Stay committed to driving the line until your dog enters the tunnel.

Driving the Line

Step 4

At this step, you will add another obstacle—another tunnel—before the discrimination (shown in Figure 10.6). (See Photo 10.C.)

1. Lead out so that you are able to drive the line rather than being left in the dust. Even if your dog gets ahead of you, continue to use your hand to push on his path.

2. Stay committed to driving the line until your dog enters the tunnel. (See Photo 10.D.) This means that your feet and shoulders must continue to face the tunnel until he vanishes. Remember that if you rotate too quickly, he can easily pull back. I have seen this hundreds of times when students practice this skill.

Step 5

Try removing the gate. Repeat the same exercise, driving the line to the tunnel. If your dog makes a single error to take the A-frame, put the gate back on.

Step 6

Add more obstacles as indicated in Figure 10.6 until you are running the whole circle starting at the jump. The more speed your dog generates, the bigger the challenge.

Step 7

Set up an alternate configuration in which your dog must now drive past the tunnel to the contact. (See Figure 10.7.) Use your gate across the tunnel initially if you need it.

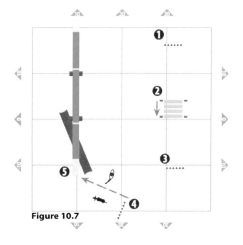

Figure 10.7

Driving the Line Issues

If your dog "accidentally" gets on the contact when you are driving the line to the tunnel, it is very important that you let him finish that obstacle with confidence. Don't blame him. Don't cause him to turn around or leap off. Don't say anything negative because you don't want to shake his initiative on contacts. Do ask him to perform his contact behavior at the end. If this situation arises, I just verbally reinforce the contact with a "Good job." Keep in mind that the dog

---

Arm and Hand Position

There are two styles of the arm and hand used when driving the line. Some handlers open their palm and use a pushing motion toward the dog. However, many handlers now prefer to keep their arm and hand low, based on a belief that this is easier for the dog to see. With the arm held low, the handler is also able to give an extra push into the dog's path if needed.

thinks that he has done the right thing. If you just let him blast off the end, his contact behavior will quickly deteriorate. When he has finished the contact, take him back to the beginning of the exercise and set up the situation so that he gets the tunnel.

Mental Practice

Here is a final sequence for you to consider. This was a challenge encountered on a United States Dog Agility Association (USDAA) intermediate course. Where is the location where you would need to drive the line? Why is this section particularly challenging?

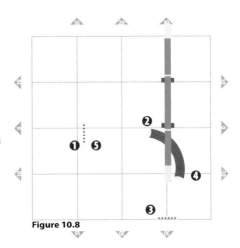

Answer: Most folks began this challenging section by front crossing jump #3. This put the dogs on the handlers' right hand and allowed them to drive the line out to tunnel #4. This would have been a good challenge even if the tunnel had been even with the dogwalk, but because the tunnel was depressed, the dogs had a good long time to look at the dogwalk. Many handlers who quit driving the line too early saw their dogs scamper up the dogwalk.

Figure 10.8

Concluding Thoughts

When you are walking courses at a trial, you will often see logjams of people. Inevitably, the handlers are milling about and contemplating how to handle a challenging discrimination. Learning to handle them confidently is at the heart of agility.

Remember that your dog is making a decision about which obstacle to take while running at full speed. Do your best to develop consistent communication, which gives him time to react as you want.

11 False Turn

I n this chapter, we will focus on another discrete skill you will find useful in handling discriminations: the false turn. In Chapter 12, we will pull all of the skills together to handle a variety of sequences in which dogs must actively choose between two or more obstacles.

Let's look at a sequence in Figure 11.1, which looks deceptively simple at first. Consider the fact that your dog is approaching the tunnel at high speed having no idea which end he is supposed to take. You might think of using a front cross between the broad jump and jump #4, but this is unlikely to work well because of the angle of jump #5. There are two other choices. The first is to run sharply to your left as your dog commits to jump #4. This may pull your dog to the correct end, but it requires you to run way off to the side, and it leaves you behind your dog. Figure 11.2 illustrates how wide you must run to use this strategy. You can see how unlikely it is that you could reverse course and get to your dog before he exits the tunnel. If you are not lined up with the weaves when your dog emerges, the odds are high that he will miss the weave pole entry.

The second and best choice is called the false turn, which is the strongest method you can use to pull your dog toward you without running off to the side. This maneuver is specifically

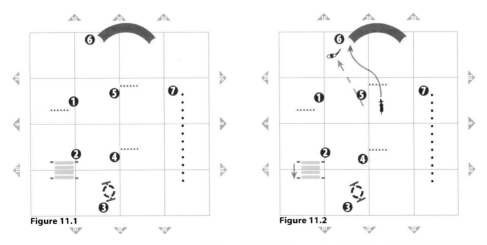

Figure 11.1   **Figure 11.2**

designed to quickly change your dog's path so that he focuses on performing the correct obstacle while you stay in a good position to handle subsequent obstacles. In a sense, it is based on fooling your dog for just a moment.

Prerequisite Skills

There are two skills that should be in place before you start to work on the false turn.

1. This strategy is based on your dog's understanding of the front cross. Although you are not executing a complete front cross, your dog must read the front cross communication and begin to turn for the false turn to work.
2. You should be comfortable with the rear cross. You will not need to rear cross every time you use a false turn, but sometimes it is necessary.

Locating the False Turn

Before we get started with teaching the false turn, there is one more important note: Where you actually perform the false turn may also determine its success. If you execute this maneuver too early, it may not clarify things for your dog. On Figure 11.3, you will see that the dog has pulled toward the handler, but he is so far from the tunnel that he could easily take either end.

The key is to wait a bit longer to direct your dog so that when you complete your false turn, your dog is closer to the correct choice. Figure 11.4 is a good example of the handler getting closer to the tunnel before telling the dog what to do.

Naturally, learning to do this in the correct spot without letting your dog choose either end of the tunnel takes lots of practice. For blistering-fast dogs, you will have to execute the turn sooner. It will help if you maintain some lateral distance in the direction you want to go because this provides the dog with a second piece of information about the correct direction. With moderately fast dogs, you can get a bit closer to the obstacle before you do the false turn because they can change directions easier.

I am often asked if the false turn will work if the dog is ahead of you. The answer is yes, if you provide adequate training as described. Because dogs have a huge field of vision, they can see

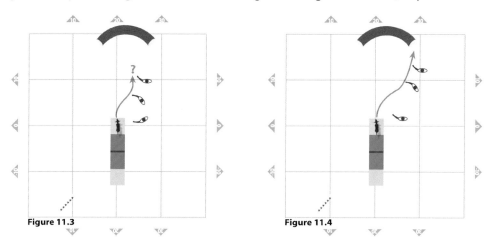

Figure 11.3   Figure 11.4

Intermediate Handling Skills

11.A

11.B

11.C

11.A: As the dog approaches the tunnel with no idea which end to take, the handler decelerates and rotates as if she is going to front cross.
11.B: This move pulls the dog off the incorrect end of the tunnel.
11.C: As soon as the dog changes direction, the handler rotates back and cues him to the correct end of the tunnel.

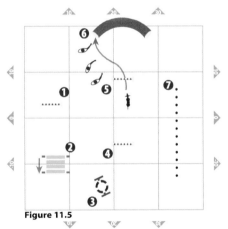

Figure 11.5

your rotation even if you are behind, assuming that they are looking for it.

Teaching the False Turn

To perform the false turn, you are going to start a front cross as if you are changing directions. This will pull your dog toward you. The second he changes his path, you will rotate back in the original direction and direct your dog to the correct obstacle. Figure 11.5 illustrates this maneuver. As you can see, this leaves the handler in a much better position to get out to the weaves successfully.

Now let's look at several photos of the false turn in action. As the dog approaches the tunnel with no idea of which end to take, the handler decelerates and rotates as if she is going to front cross. (See Photo 11.A.) This move pulls her dog off the wrong end of the tunnel. (See Photo 11.B.) As soon as the dog changes direction, the handler rotates back and cues the dog to the correct end of the tunnel. (See Photo 11.C.)

The challenge of this move is that the handler's rotation must be very quick—lightening fast, in fact. Otherwise, the dog will come back too far in the wrong direction, which adds time. When a handler rotates back and forward too slowly, it is known as holding on too long. You will notice in

False Turn

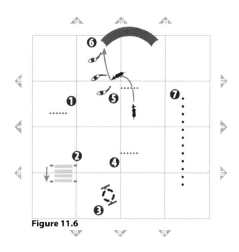

Figure 11.6

Figure 11.6, which shows a handler holding on too long, the dog ends up facing the wrong direction. Done correctly, the false turn should pull the dog toward you and correct his path but not completely pull him around in the wrong direction.

There are seven steps to teaching your dog to read and react to the false turn.

Step 1

To begin, review the front cross to remind your dog that he should curve toward you when you switch hands and begin your rotation. (See Chapter 7.) Set up two jumps in a straight line a comfortable distance apart.

1. Lead out past the first jump with your dog on your left. Have a cookie or toy in your right hand.
2. Release your dog over the jumps. As he commits to the second jump, start your rotation as if you are front crossing, but stay in the same spot.
3. After he clears the second jump, he will curve toward you because he knows how to read the cues for a front cross. Deliver your cookie. (See Photo 11.D.)
4. Repeat several times.

Step 2

Now you will add two other obstacles. You can use any obstacles, but Figure 11.7 features a simple setup that works well.

1. Put your dog on a *stay*, and lead out between jumps #1 and #2.
2. Call your dog. Execute your false turn to pull him toward you. Then cue him to take the tunnel. (See Photos 11.E and 11.F.) You will note that the handler in these photos only needs a subtle front cross to cue her dog to pull toward her. Experiment to see how far you need to rotate to get your dog to curve toward you.
3. Repeat several times.

Step 3

Next, increase the difficulty by tempting your dog with an obstacle straight ahead, but use the false turn to get him onto the correct path for the next obstacle. (See Figure 11.8.) Move your

Intermediate Handling Skills

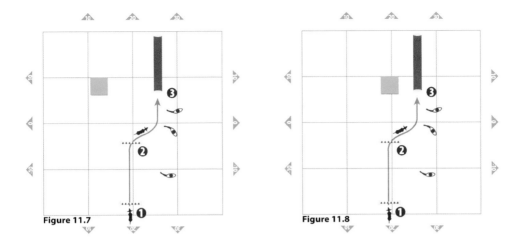

Figure 11.7   Figure 11.8

jump or table onto a straight line with the first two jumps. Remember to keep handling this with your dog on your left.

After a couple of runs to the tunnel, start alternating between the obstacle straight ahead and the offset obstacle. This will keep you and your dog from going on autopilot.

Step 4
Now redo each of the steps starting with your dog on your right and executing your false turn to get the correct obstacle. (See Photo 11.G.)

Step 5
Start to substitute other obstacles as shown in Figure 11.9, which features a sequence with an A-frame and teeter. Use your gate across the A-frame, if necessary, to help your dog be successful initially. Reinforce generously when he gets the teeter.

Step 6
Up to this point, you have been able to lead out and perform all of these false turns from a standstill. Now you should start to include this type of challenge in the middle of larger sequences so that you must do them on the fly. The sequence in Figure 11.10 requires that you use your false turn to line up your dog with the broad jump. You could, of course, substitute any other obstacle.

Field of Vision
Dogs have a much wider field of vision than humans do. Although breeds vary, scientists estimate that all dogs have a range of vision somewhere between 240 and 270 degrees. Although they are quite nearsighted and their range of color is not as great as humans', they balance this by an ability to see in much dimmer light than we do. All in all, they see quite well enough to read your cues on the agility course.

False Turn

11.D: As your dog commits to the second jump, rotate as if you are front crossing, but stay in the same spot and deliver a cookie.

11.E and 11.F: Call your dog, execute your false turn to pull him toward you, and cue him to take the tunnel.

11.G: Redo each of the steps, starting with your dog on your right and executing your false turn to get the correct obstacle.

Step 7

Tunnels present one of the more interesting uses of the false turn because most dogs love tunnels and run at them so enthusiastically. The exercise in Figure 11.11 is perfect for teaching your dog that you will tell him which end to take. Practice both sequences with the dog on your right and then on your left. If he struggles with this, increase the distance between the jump and the tunnel. Decrease the distance when he understands the game.

False Turn Issues

The false turn is a powerful and useful strategy. The danger is that some dogs get wise to this moment of deception. If you use the false turn too often, you may possibly create a dog who doesn't change directions when you front cross because he thinks that you are really going to rotate back in the original direction.

It is relatively easy to prevent this situation by alternating the false turn regularly with real front crosses. That way, your dog will learn to watch and react to you correctly rather than assuming that he can outguess you.

Intermediate Handling Skills

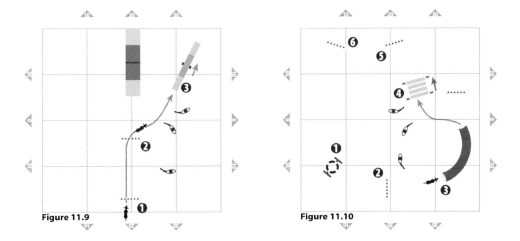

Figure 11.9

Figure 11.10

Mental Practice

The sequence in Figure 11.12 has one place where a false turn might be useful. Identify that place. Why is this maneuver a good idea here?

Answer: The false turn would be executed between the tunnel and jump #4. Because the dog comes out of the tunnel looking at both the tire and the jump, the handler needs to make a strong move to pull him to the correct obstacle. A false turn will leave the handler in the best position to handle the obstacles that follow.

Concluding Thoughts

With the addition of the false turn, you now have seven strategies for handling those pesky discriminations that you are going to encounter on intermediate courses. We will review the complete list in the next chapter. Your next challenge is to learn to analyze a course and choose the best strategy or strategies to help your dog select the correct obstacle when the choice is not immediately obvious.

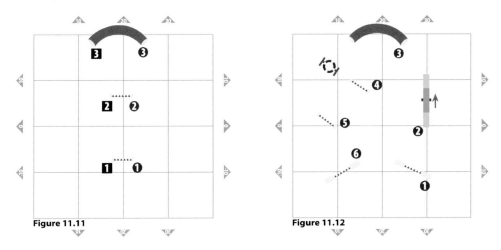

Figure 11.11

Figure 11.12

False Turn

12 Discriminations

I once saw a video taken from a camera that had been attached to a dog's collar while he ran an agility course. The pace was blistering. The obstacles were a blur. It is easy to forget that our dogs are running as fast as they can run and making continuous decisions about what to do based on our body language and verbal cues. After seeing this video, it seems amazing to me that our dogs are able to do what they do on a simple agility course. It's absolutely miraculous that, on intermediate courses, they can "read" what we are telling them and make a split second decision between two obstacles positioned side by side.

One difference I notice between less experienced handlers and intermediate handlers is that novice folks often see only one option for handling a discrimination, while intermediates consider a range of options and select the one that is the best fit for their dog. More advanced handlers also consider the obstacles that follow the discrimination and whether the strategy they select will leave them in a good spot to handle them efficiently. As we proceed through a series of examples, work on building your flexibility by looking at all of your options for handling each sequence, and then select the one that seems best for the situation and your dog.

This chapter is about learning to select the best strategies to give your dog clear and timely information so that when he encounters those discriminations, he can make the correct, high-speed choice.

Prerequisite Skills
You already have a variety of skills that you will utilize in working discriminations:
- lateral distance
- speed changes
- front cross
- rear cross
- shoulder pull

12.A: Elevate your outside hand for just a moment to tell your dog to take the closer obstacle.

- driving the line
- false turn

I recommend two new things to students when we are handling two obstacles placed in close proximity. These are used only when you want the dog to take the obstacle closest to you. First, I suggest that they use their dog's name every time. Because you don't use a dog's name often in agility, he tends to hear it when you do. Once he understands that you will say it only when you want him to work the obstacle next to you, he will read that cue easily. Second, you might find it useful to elevate your outside hand for just a moment to tell your dog to take the closer obstacle. (See Photo 12.A.) There is no other time in agility that both hands are used at once, so this cue provides a clear, unique message.

Teaching Yourself to Handle Discriminations

Now let's take a look at a series of discriminations and consider the handling options. We will start with one that requires the closer obstacle so that you can see how your older skills and new skills can be combined.

In each of the scenarios that follow, I will take you inside the intermediate handler's brain. I believe that it is useful to understand

Take Note
When you are working discriminations in class and there are two ways to handle a sequence, ask your teacher if you can run it twice and try each approach. If we get only one chance, we generally select the skill that we are most comfortable with rather than expanding our toolbox. Ask your teacher and classmates to watch both strategies and give you feedback about which one communicated most clearly to your dog.

Intermediate Handling Skills

how experienced handlers think about each discrimination and make a decision about what they will do. I have edited out any thoughts they might have about their friend's new green running shoes or the gophers that are popping out of their holes at the edge of the course.

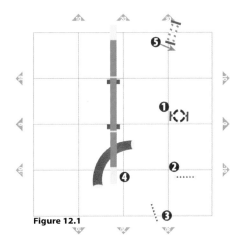

Figure 12.1

Sequence A

The sequence in Figure 12.1 highlights a discrimination in which you ask your dog to take the obstacle closest to you. It is harder than some discriminations that combine a contact and tunnel because jump #3 is so close and gives the handler less time to pull her dog into the contact.

You will notice that in this intermediate handler's thinking, she decides to use five skills: *This is a tough corner. My dog's path is from that jump right into the tunnel. What can I do here to pull him to the dogwalk? I can use my lateral distance. As I round the corner, I need to stay away from the dogwalk. If I push in too far, I will push him into the tunnel. I am also going to use a speed change to pull him toward me. As soon as he commits to jump #3, I am going to hesitate for just a second to pull him toward me. I also need to turn my feet and shoulders right away too to pull him around the corner. Is there anything else I can do to cue him? I am also going to raise my second hand briefly and say his name so that he knows exactly what I want.*

Check that you can identify the five skills put into action. They are lateral distance, a speed change, a shoulder pull, use of the dog's name, and a cue with the second hand.

Sequence B

The intermediate sequence in Figure 12.2 appeared in a recent trial. As the dog came around the corner, he needed to choose between the incorrect tunnel and the correct weave poles. There are two dramatically different ways to handle this discrimination. What are your two options to help your dog select the weaves?

The two choices you should consider in this case are lateral distance with a shoulder pull or a front cross. Let's explore how you might think through this challenge and make your decision: *This is the hardest part on this course. My dog will be coming around the corner from jump #3 very quickly. His path is liable to be wide, which will put him on*

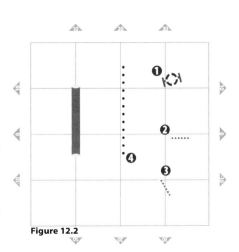

Figure 12.2

Discriminations

a line to the tunnel, an off course. My dog really likes tunnels, so I am going to have to work this carefully. I think I could handle this two ways. I could stay well to the right of the weave poles as my dog rounds the corner and turn my feet and shoulders quickly toward the weaves. This might pull him in toward the weaves. Or I could front cross between the jump and weaves to get my dog on my right and push him into the poles. Which will work better? If I try to pull him to the poles and his momentum is too fast, I am not sure if he will make the turn. I may even block his view of the poles. On the other hand, if I front cross, he will be able to see the poles easily and I will be able to push toward him strongly to hold him out of the tunnel. Okay, that is what I'll do.

In reality, handlers tried both strategies. Most handlers who tried a shoulder pull with lateral distance to draw the dog to the weaves saw their dogs vanish into the tunnel. Those who front crossed between jump #3 and the weaves had a high rate of success. Although you will not always make the correct decision about which strategy to use in handling discriminations, you can increase your percentage of good choices with practice.

Sequence C

There are two clear options for handling the sequence in Figure 12.3 as well. What are they? Remember to consider which choice will leave you in the best position to handle the obstacle after the tunnel.

If you answered that either the rear cross or the front cross could be used, you are correct. You might think about the discrimination like this: *I could do a couple of things here. I might use a shoulder pull to help my dog find the tunnel and then rear cross to get to jump #5. The second option is to front cross between jump #3 and the tunnel. If I pull my dog to the tunnel and rear cross, it is a very sharp cross and I could pull him out of the tunnel. It would also leave me in a bad spot to handle jump #5. If I decelerate and front cross between the jump and tunnel, I can push him toward the tunnel nicely and then easily make it out to handle jump #5.*

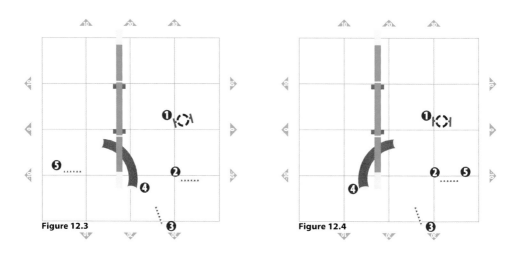

Figure 12.3   Figure 12.4

Intermediate Handling Skills

Intermediates consider a range of options when handling discriminations and select the one that is the best fit for their dog.

Although handlers tried both of these strategies, the success rate was considerably higher for those who did the front cross. It mattered where the handler front crossed—those who followed the front cross rule about positioning and crossed very closely to the tunnel got a tight line from their dog with no confusion about the dogwalk at all.

Sequence D

The sequence in Figure 12.4 starts the same as in Sequence C but requires a different strategy. Although there is only one possible strategy here, this is a good time to remember that you should mentally and physically review what you will do to cue your dog.

Your thinking might sound like this: *Is there any way to handle this discrimination other than driving the line to the tunnel? No. I need to make sure that I look only at the tunnel and not glance at the dogwalk at all. I must be sure not to turn my feet and shoulders before he is well into that tunnel. There is no hurry. There is plenty of time to get out to handle jump #5.*

Sequence E

The sequence in Figure 12.5 is a bit different. Taken from a recent trial, the discrimination is between an obstacle that requires a wide turn and an attractive obstacle straight ahead. Whenever your dog is approaching a tunnel at high speed and is not supposed to take it, it presents an interesting challenge. In this case, there are two clear options for handling. What are they, and

111

Discriminations

which has the greatest chance of keeping your dog out of the tunnel?

Here is one handler's thinking: *That tunnel is really obvious, and my dog loves tunnels. How can I keep him out of there? I could front cross after jump #2 and pull him around the corner from jump #4 to jump #5. I would have to make sure that I stay lateral and not drive too far in toward that tunnel. Or I could keep him on my right and rear cross jump #4. That would get me behind him, but he always knows that we are changing direction when I rear cross. That might be the stronger move if I cross and drive quickly toward the next jump.*

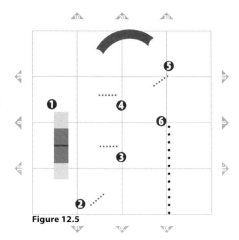

Figure 12.5

This was a case in which both strategies worked if they were executed well. Handlers' decisions were based entirely on the skill that worked best for their dog. Handlers who used lateral distance with a shoulder pull to get their dogs around the corner on their left were a bit quicker. However, several lost dogs into the tunnel if the handler hesitated or looked at the tunnel. The rear cross was a bit slower, but virtually no dog went off course.

Discrimination Issues

The biggest challenge I observe as students learn to handle discriminations is to remember to handle them with purpose and precision. There is a tendency to run toward two obstacles yelling the name of the correct obstacle rather than using the specific skills we have been talking about. This rarely works. As you walk a sequence or course, plan every detail of how you will communicate with your dog at each discrimination so that he performs the correct obstacle.

Mental Practice

There are two sequences for you to think about in Figure 12.6. They include tunnel/contact discriminations as well as discriminations between other obstacles. How would you handle them?

Answer: The red circle exercise starts with an obvious discrimination between the A-frame and the tunnel. Imagine yourself staying very lateral of the A-frame, hesitating slightly, saying

Line of Sight
Dogs know what you are looking at. This is amazing but true. If you look at the incorrect obstacle in a discrimination, you greatly increase the odds that your dog will take it, and you will end up with an off course. Train yourself to look at only the obstacle that you want your dog to perform.

Intermediate Handling Skills

your dog's name as he rounds the corner and raising your second hand very briefly. After the A-frame, did you see the discrimination between the tire and table? A front cross at the bottom of the A-frame would be a good strategy so that you could push your dog to the table. After the table, you should have pushed your dog into tunnel #5 using your left hand. A front cross at jump #6 will pull the dog back to another contact/tunnel discrimination.

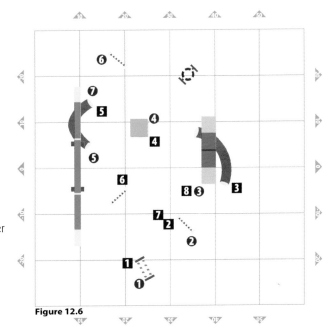

The blue squares reverse the opening discrimination. A strategic lead out is important here so that you can pick up your dog and drive the line into tunnel #3. This time a

Figure 12.6

shoulder pull to the table will work. Drive the line between the table and tunnel #5. Don't run too far forward and inadvertently cue the dogwalk. As you round the corner to the A-frame, use your deceleration and lateral distance to cue that you want the closer obstacle. You may bring your second hand up briefly and use your dog's name.

Concluding Thoughts

I have mentioned several times that it is your goal to build a system of communication so that your dog knows exactly what you are telling him. There is no place where that is more important than discriminations. Your dog should not have to hesitate while he figures out what you want because your movements are consistent, timely, and crisp.

If at any time your dog struggles with doing the "right" thing, take some time to help him understand. For example, my young Sheltie had a hard time taking the dogwalk if there was a tunnel beyond, such as in Sequence A. I taught him using a very low-tech method. I loaded my hand close to him with cookies and asked him to come around the corner slowly. I then dropped treats to create a yellow brick road to the dogwalk. We did this a number of times, increasing speed slowly. Once he understood the game, I began to use the skills we've discussed, such as lateral distance, a speed change, and his name. He learned to love the discrimination game without ever losing confidence.

Discriminations

13 Serpentines

When you look at an agility course, it is easy to see each obstacle as a separate entity—here a jump, there a jump. However, it is often more useful to see certain obstacles as clusters. This will allow you to make strategic decisions about how to handle the cluster efficiently.

One type of cluster that you will encounter frequently as an intermediate handler is called a serpentine. You can identify a serpentine with one simple rule: You could handle the cluster by front crossing on both sides of the middle obstacle. Take a look at this classic three-jump serpentine. I have indicated where you could front cross on each side of the second jump.

This is not to say that you want to front cross every time you have your dog do a serpentine. You may do this sometimes depending on the location of the obstacles that follow the serpentine, but there is another way to handle many serpentines that you will be learning in this chapter that requires no crossing on your part.

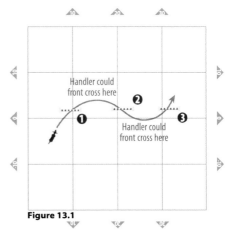

Figure 13.1

For those of you who are horse people, there is a second way to identify a serpentine. During the configuration on Figure 13.1, you will notice that the dog must change leads, from right to left, to make the turn from jump #2 to jump #3. Depending on the approach to the serpentine, some may require two lead changes. With good serpentine handling, your dog will learn to anticipate the lead changes and execute them with little effort.

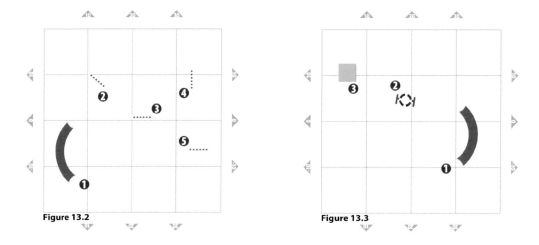

Figure 13.2

Figure 13.3

Not all serpentines are as obvious as the first example. On the sequence in Figure 13.2, jumps #2 through #4 are a serpentine. You can tell because you could handle this by front crossing before and after jump #3. Keep in mind that you may not want to handle the serpentine that way, but you could. Also, any obstacles can be configured to create a serpentine. Figure 13.3 is an example that includes the tire and table.

When you are walking sequences, keep your eye out for serpentines. As you will learn, handing obstacles as a serpentine can simplify complex sections of a course.

Prerequisite Skills

Before you start the serpentine, your dog must first know how to handle a 180-degree turn. If he is familiar with looking for a jump that is not obvious, this process will go more quickly.

Teaching the Serpentine

In the past, the handler made a lot of dramatic moves, including turning backward to pull the dog over the middle jump, to get her dog through a serpentine. Those days are over. Of all of the changes in agility in recent years, it is easy to argue that the new method of handling the serpentine is the most significant. The strategy you are going to learn is much faster and clearer to the dog. If you have learned the older method, you will have to do a bit of unlearning. If you are new to the serpentine, it will take some work to master this maneuver, but in the end, you will learn to love it.

To introduce your dog to serpentines, we are going to follow a sequential process. At times, it may be hard to see how the pieces fit together. Stick with me—I have used this in many classes and watched students become serpentine stars. I also just completed this process with my young Border Collie and am enjoying the results.

Step 1

In this exercise, you will learn to get in the correct position and how to use your body to

Intermediate Handling Skills

cue your dog to curve toward you and take the obstacle between you and him. Your dog will learn how to read that communication. It is important to teach him specifically how to handle the middle jump in the serpentine, which is the trickiest obstacle. If mishandled, your dog will run right past it because it is easier than making the turn to come toward you.

1. Set up one jump. Position your dog at an angle to the jump as if he were coming around the corner from another obstacle.
2. Position yourself at the second stanchion. Have a toy or cookie in the hand farthest from your dog.
3. Rotate only your upper body so that the reinforcement is at your hip. (See Photo 13.A.) Your feet should continue to face toward the spot where the third obstacle will be.
4. Most handlers call their dogs over the second jump. You can use your pup's name or a directional word such as "here." This provides one more piece of information for your dog.
5. Release him to jump using whatever verbal command you plan to use.
6. As soon as he lands, give him the cookie or play a quick game of tug. (See Photo 13.B.) If he has trouble stopping at your side, take one or two steps forward so that he has room to stop right next to you.

Step 2

Once your dog is coming in over the middle jump and into your side, it is time to add another obstacle in the serpentine. This will ultimately be the third obstacle. (It is easier to master the handling of the second and third obstacles in the serpentine and then add the first obstacle, which presents the greatest challenge.)

Position the new jump as pictured in Figure 13.4. The jump is angled initially so that the dog can find it easily.

1. Put your dog on a *stay* behind the middle jump. From the other side at the second stanchion, call him over using the upper body rotation you have been practicing.
2. As soon as he commits to the second jump, start driving forward and cue him to take the third jump using the hand closest to him. (See Photo 13.C.) If at any time he starts missing the middle jump, you have moved forward before he committed to taking it. Slow down just a bit until he understands the game thoroughly.
3. Gradually rotate the third jump until it is in a line with your original jump (the one that will soon be the middle jump).

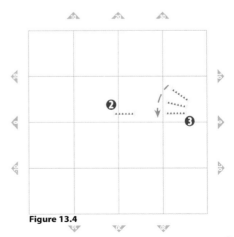

Figure 13.4

Serpentines

13.A: Rotate only your upper body so that the reinforcement is at your hip.

13.B: As soon as your dog lands, give him the cookie.

13.C: When he commits to the second jump, drive forward toward the third jump.

Step 3

Once your dog is comfortably coming in over the second jump and pushing out over the third jump, it is time to add the first jump, as pictured in Figure 13.5. Set it at about 145 degrees to the second jump so that your dog doesn't have to work too hard to find the second jump.

1. Send your dog over the first jump. (See Photo 13.D.) Hold him out using your arm as you would on a 180-degree turn. As he makes the arc, slide over to the second stanchion of the second jump. Rotate back with your upper body to cue your dog to come in and take that jump. (See Photo 13.E.)

2. The first couple of times, you can lure your dog in over the second jump with your cookie or toy in your hand, but quickly drop that and reward him after he takes the jump.

3. Drive forward toward the third jump and have your dog take the final jump in the serpentine. (See Photo 13.F.) Keep moving forward past the third jump so that he doesn't knock that bar.

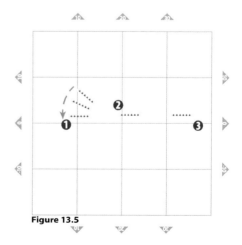

Figure 13.5

Intermediate Handling Skills

4. Gradually rotate the first jump until it forms a straight line with the other two obstacles. Continue to reinforce if your dog reads your cue and comes in over the second obstacle.

It takes considerable self-control for a dog to arc in and take the second jump in a serpentine. It is much easier to just run straight ahead and pass the second jump altogether. If your dog starts to miss the middle obstacle, just focus on the first and second obstacles for a while. Don't drive on to the third obstacle. This will generally keep you from blasting forward so fast that the dog doesn't have time to find the middle jump. Once he genuinely understands that your cue (upper body rotation) means that he should always take the middle obstacle coming toward you, you can add the third obstacle again.

As you work on this third step, your path should be parallel with the jumps, and you should be quite close to the jumps. (See Figure 13.6.) Because you have taught your dog well to read your cues, you don't need to weave in and out yourself.

This is a useful time to bring in a friend to watch and give feedback so that you can check that you are proceeding correctly. As your dog takes the second jump, he should be coming in

13.D: Send your dog over the first jump.

13.E: Rotate your upper body back to cue him to come in.

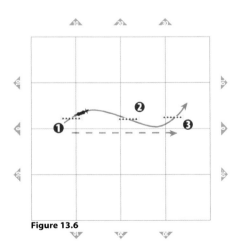

Figure 13.6

13.F: Drive forward toward the third jump.

Serpentines

Breaking Down Complex Tasks
Good trainers find ways to split complex tasks into understandable pieces for their dogs. Once the dog understands each component of the behavior, they can be chained together into a lovely final product. The serpentine training in this chapter is a classic case of splitting a challenging maneuver into several steps so that your dog can understand each part before tackling the whole. Trying to teach any complex behavior as a single "lump" will leave both you and your dog frustrated.

behind you because you are standing at the second stanchion. Make sure that you are not stopping in the middle of the jump and blocking his path. Also check that you are not stopping at the first stanchion. This means that he would land in front of you, a position that would make it impossible to push him to the third obstacle in the serpentine.

Step 4
When your dog is comfortable with performing the three-jump serpentine with the obstacles in a straight line, vary the distance between obstacles. Obstacle spacing will challenge different types of dogs. For example, a toy dog may find a serpentine in which the obstacles are spread out most difficult because he has to run a distance to find the next obstacle. In contrast, a dog with a big and/or fast stride may find a serpentine with tightly placed obstacles most challenging because he is required to change his lead on the landing stride or the stride following the landing stride.

Step 5
Make sure to practice the serpentine going in the other direction, from right to left. Remember that you will switch from your right hand to your left hand briefly when you are providing the cue for your dog to come in over the second jump.

Step 6
Now you can get creative with your serpentines. Incorporate other obstacles and change the configurations so that they are less obvious. You can always check that you have created a serpentine by applying the front cross rules we talked about earlier in this chapter.

Teaching the Serpentine With the Front Cross
There are times when it makes more sense to do a front cross in handling a serpentine, generally if there is a strong pull after the last obstacle in the serpentine. Take a look at Figure 13.7, a sequence in which the serpentine precedes the A-frame.

In this case, a front cross makes the most sense because it puts you in the best position to pull your dog tightly between jump #5 and the A-frame. Remember to review the rules for front crosses from Chapter 7.

Serpentine Issues
Serpentine handling, at its best, is complex. Handlers are prone to making two mistakes. The first is

Intermediate Handling Skills

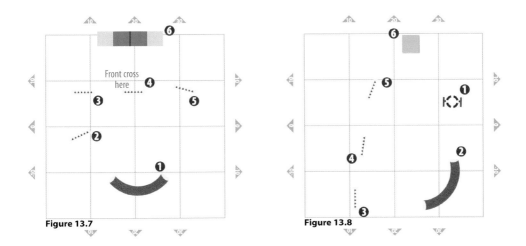

Figure 13.7

Figure 13.8

that they forget to use their upper body rotation cue to invite the dog in over the middle obstacle. This leaves them trying to steer using only the hand closest to the dog, which we use in most other instances. Unfortunately, this does not give the dog enough information, and he often skips the second jump. The second issue is that handlers often move too slowly between obstacles #1 and #2. This means that their dogs get ahead of them, which makes it nearly impossible to push out to the third obstacle. Once you send your dog over the first obstacle, it is time for warp speed. If you accelerate to the second jump, you will beat your dog because he is traveling a much longer path. Once you are ahead of your dog, the skills you have been learning will allow you to pick him up smoothly, as you have been practicing, and direct him over the third obstacle.

Mental Practice

Figure 13.8 features a longer sequence with a three-jump serpentine. Where would you position yourself to handle jump #4? What are your arms doing? What is your upper body doing? What are your feet doing? When would you start driving toward jump #5?

Answer: For the serpentine, send your dog over jump #3 and keep your arm up to hold him out. Then slide across to the farthest stanchion of jump #4 to clear his path. Your arm switch should be from left to right to cue him to come in and over the middle jump of the serpentine. Your upper body should rotate back during the arm change while your feet continue to point at jump #5. As soon as your dog commits to jump #4 but has not yet jumped, start driving toward jump #5 so that he knows exactly where to go when he lands.

Concluding Thoughts

Smooth serpentines take lots of practice, both to understand the timing and to get in the correct position. Remember not to overwork your dog and to end your session while he is still having fun. It is lovely to recognize a serpentine when you encounter it and to feel completely confident that you and your dog can handle it.

14

Weave Pole Entries

I n teaching the weave poles, you have undoubtedly learned that they are a complex obstacle requiring a great deal of understanding from dogs. At the novice level, most handlers get into the habit of escorting their dog right to the poles. This is possible because most novice-level entries to the poles are relatively straight.

At the intermediate level, those days are over. Dogs must learn to enter the poles from a variety of angles that challenge their understanding of the job. Figure 14.1 features an example of one type of intermediate weave pole entry that requires the dog to travel out and around the first pole.

You may also find yourself faced with sequences that lead your dog toward an incorrect entry. To be successful, he must have a firm understanding that it is his job to find the entry between the first and second poles no matter how hard he has to work. Take a look at the example in Figure 14.2.

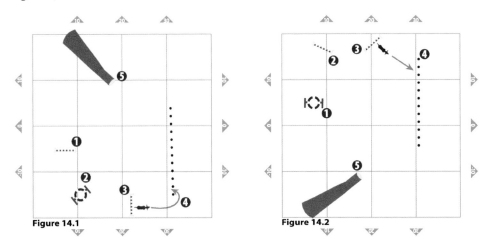

Figure 14.1

Figure 14.2

It is ideal to start with wide guides, such as garden fencing or exercise pens, that can be wired to the poles.

In this chapter, we'll take a look at teaching your dog to handle these types of entries. My goal is that you can tell your pup to weave from any angle, and he will seek out the poles and enter correctly without you escorting him. This skill will definitely elevate your game to the next level.

Prerequisite Skills

We will be using a tool called weave pole guides, which were discussed in *The Beginner's Guide to Dog Agility*. The guides, or wires as they are often called, will provide visual and physical support to your dog when he is performing the poles. If, by chance, you taught him to weave without guides, you may want to introduce them now. There are many types of guides, from thin plastic wires to inexpensive plastic garden fencing. Dogs generally learn to accept the guides after a few opportunities to run through, even if they have never seen them before. The guides will help your dog to do the poles correctly at full speed even as the difficulty increases.

Using weave pole guides is so important because dogs have a tendency to pattern on behaviors very quickly. If a dog does the weave poles incorrectly even two times in a session, he will believe that this is the correct behavior. Then it will take numerous repetitions to get him back on the right path. It is much smarter to help a dog pattern the correct behavior than try to fix something that has gone wrong.

It is ideal to start the game with wide guides, such as garden fencing or exercise pens, that can be wired to the poles. This eliminates the temptation to jump out of the channel. As your dog understands the game, you will want to switch to the narrow guides from plastic or PVC. In the

Intermediate Handling Skills

exercises that follow, I will suggest using fencing until you go through as many as seven steps before you switch to narrow guides. You may choose to switch earlier, but be careful that your dog doesn't start leaping out.

You can start weave pole entry work with young pups or with dogs who are already weaving independently without guides. However, with pups, you should keep the channel open so that they don't have to actually weave. Once the growth plates close, you can easily progress to the next steps. If you have an experienced dog who is weaving slowly or is dependent on you to escort him to the poles, you might start at the beginning with a wide channel and reteach him to take responsibility for finding the poles and moving through with enthusiasm.

Teaching the Weave Pole Entry
Step 1

1. Use a set of channel weaves with guides on. Set the channel wide so that your dog doesn't have to push through even if he has been working on straight poles. You want your dog to focus on entries initially and not worry about weaving.

> **Take Note**
> As with other aspects of agility, new methods continue to show promise. A dramatically different and exciting approach, called the "2 x 2 method," was developed by Susan Garrett. Using this method, dogs are learning their weaves more quickly than by traditional methods. You can explore this approach by viewing Susan's DVD *2x2 Weave Training*.

2. To make sure that your dog is comfortable with the equipment, put him through the channel a couple of times by escorting him to the entry and walking quickly alongside. Remember that you want to pause until he finds his entry and then accelerate until you are next to his head.

3. If your dog gets ahead of you, toss his toy ahead once he finishes the channel so that he runs straight ahead rather than curving back toward you. If your dog is slower than you want, feel free to race ahead and call him as long as he doesn't jump out of the channel.

Do this exercise with your dog on both sides.

Step 2

As soon as your dog is comfortable with running through the channel to earn his reward, you are going to ask him to become independent. When I do this in classes, even with inexperienced dogs, this takes very little time.

1. Start at a distance of about 10 feet (3 m) from the poles with your dog on your left, and walk quietly toward the poles. (See Photo 14.A.) Look at them, not at your dog. Say nothing, and don't move your arms. He will try to figure out what to do. (You can stay close to the poles the first time or two so that he sees where you are headed.)

2. As soon as he ducks into the channel, mark it with a "Yes!" and move forward quickly. (See Photo 14.B.)

3. Reinforce generously by tossing a cookie or toy forward after each repetition as soon as your dog exits the channel so that he doesn't curve toward you.

Weave Pole Entries

4. Repeat several times.

Gradually increase your lateral distance from the poles so that your dog has to move away from you to enter them. (See Photo 14.C.) This may be hard for you if you are in the habit of escorting your dog, but let him learn his job without interference. If he gets confused, you may have moved away too quickly. Do this in small incremental steps.

Remember that you should never come to a standstill when approaching the poles. However, do your best to resist the urge to rush right up to the poles so that your dog gets comfortable with lateral distance.

Step 3

Repeat Step 2 with your dog on your right. This is just a bit more challenging because he must go out and around the first pole to enter the channel. If you start by aiming at the poles and move laterally in small increments, he will quickly understand. Remember, use your marker "yes!" every time your dog enters, and reinforce generously at the end. Dogs get very enthusiastic about this game, so you may need to restrain him by the collar if he is taking off to the poles before you are ready.

Step 4

The first three steps may take only two or three lessons. You are ready to move on as soon as your dog sees the weaves and wants to race into the channel. Now you are ready to add angled entries.

Gradually change your position by migrating to increasingly challenging spots, as indicated on Figure 14.3. (See Photo 14.D.) You can see how the dog is learning to travel away from you to find the correct entry on his own. In the last position, your dog is almost making a 180-degree turn to find the poles. Once again, remember that you must always move forward with your dog because he should stop if you stop, but go slowly so that he develops his ability to find the entry independently.

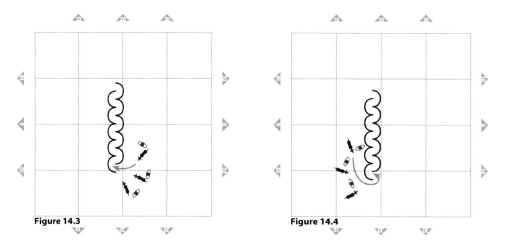

Figure 14.3   **Figure 14.4**

Intermediate Handling Skills

Step 5

Repeat Step 4 with your dog on your right. As shown in Figure 14.4, move incrementally until he is finding the weaves from 180 degrees.

Step 6

With your dog on both your right and left, add lateral distance, as demonstrated in Figure 14.5. Stay farther and farther from the poles as you work all of your angles from both sides. If at any time your dog struggles with finding the entry, make sure that you are continuing to move forward just enough to support him as he travels forward. Shorten the distance and angles if he gets confused momentarily.

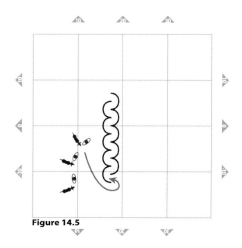

Figure 14.5

Step 7

If your pup still has open growth plates, don't proceed with this step—check with your vet about your breed. If your pup is fully mature, start moving the weave poles closer together. Do this slowly over a number of training sessions. This may take several weeks of consistent training. If your dog slows down dramatically, you have gone too fast. Continue until the poles are straight and he is finding the entry at every angle from both sides.

It is important that this exercise not just get harder and harder, or some dogs will become discouraged. Occasionally alternate the wider channel so that your pup can blast through with the tighter channel.

As the poles are lined up, you need to incorporate your ability to change speed again. As your dog approaches the poles, slow down briefly and let him drive ahead of you. This gives him time to find his entry. If you continue at the same rate of speed, it is very likely that he will come right with you and miss his entry. Once he enters the poles, accelerate to catch up with him.

Step 8

If you have been using garden fencing or exercise pens to keep your dog within the channel, swap those with less restrictive guides. (See Photo 14.E.) In the photo, you will see wires made with black irrigation hose that make a perfect transition from garden fencing to going wireless. Repeat the exercise from a variety of angles and lateral distances.

Step 9

Start to remove the guides, starting with the middle to the end. Keep the entry wires on until last to highlight the entries for your dog.

When you think that your dog is ready, remove the entry wires too. Do a challenging entry, and then put them right back on so that he feels supported. Over several weeks, alternate putting your

Weave Pole Entries

14.A: Start at a distance about 10 feet (3 m) from the poles with your dog on your left, and walk quietly toward the poles.

14.B: As soon as he ducks into the channel, mark it with a "yes!" and move forward quickly.

14.C: Gradually increase your lateral distance from the poles so that your dog has to move away from you to enter them.

14.D: Gradually change your position by migrating to increasingly challenging spots.

14.E: If you have been using garden fencing or exercise pens, switch those with less restrictive guides.

entry wires on and taking them off. For some reason, folks resist this. I want to emphasize that it is never a good idea to go cold turkey and take away a tool too quickly that you have been using to help your dog.

Step 10

Anytime you encounter a particularly difficult weave entry during your training, bring out your entry wires. Run your dog through once or twice, then take them off and do a final run. I do this with my dogs throughout their entire competitive careers just to refresh their understanding of their job with the weaves.

Intermediate Handling Skills

Weave Pole Training
It is possible to train a fine agility dog without owning agility equipment—except when it comes to weave poles. This obstacle requires training several times a week. Sessions should be no more than a couple of minutes long. Always get your dog revved up to play the weave pole game because you ultimately want him to weave at full speed.

Weave Pole Issues

It is very common to see dogs, even those who have been practicing their independent weave poles entries, miss their entries in trials. This is because the excited handler keeps running at a steady rate of speed right past the first poles. This does not give the dog any time to find his entry and steady himself in the poles. The dog sees no reason to stay in those silly poles if you are just going to leave him behind. You can easily fix this by slowing down before the first pole and giving your dog a moment to enter. As soon as he begins to weave, move up smoothly to your position across from his head.

Mental Practice

The sequence in Figure 14.6 is taken from an intermediate course at a United States Dog Agility Association (USDAA) trial. What is the specific challenge posed by this weave pole entry?

Answer: This course presented a challenging weave pole entry because the dogs had to be pulled around the corner quickly to prevent the off course over the jump straight ahead. Once the dogs saw the poles, successful handlers hesitated to let their dogs drive ahead. Then it was up to the dogs to put their understanding of the weave pole entry into action.

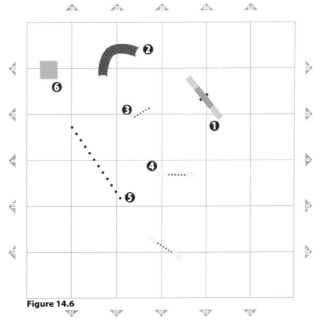

Figure 14.6

Concluding Thoughts

There is an interesting phenomenon with weave poles: Handlers often become foolishly stubborn. Even though their dog is making mistakes, they persist in trying to get him to do it correctly. Their mantra is: *I know he can do it.* That's nice, I say, but he isn't doing it. Put your wires back on. Widen the channel. If your dog gets confused at any point, help him out. Use whatever tools you need to help him get it right, and then reinforce generously. If you take your time and limit the number of mistakes your dog makes, he will reward you with a lively, reliable weave pole performance.

Weave Pole Entries

15
Getting Started on Course

There are many times that I enter the ring for a run at a trial, look at the first few obstacles, and say "Holy toledo" or something similar. Just yesterday, a group of my students, in only their second trial, came face to face with the opening in Figure 15.1.

As you can see, it takes some skill to keep the dog from racing right up the A-frame. Plenty of dogs did not make the turn to jump #3 if the handlers didn't do things perfectly. We will review later in this chapter what worked in this sequence.

In the old days of agility at the novice level, one could count on the obstacles being set in a simple straight line or curve without discriminations. Then things changed drastically as soon as you entered the intermediate ranks. Now you might encounter a tough start at any level.

There are two ways that teachers and judges arrange obstacles to increase difficulty. One type of challenge requires the dog to discriminate between two obstacles very early in the sequence. Consider both the sequence in Figure 15.1 and the sequence in Figure 15.2 from an intermediate course. The second configuration that course designers utilize to add difficulty is to set obstacles at odd angles. Figure 15.3 is a classic example in which the dog has to change directions to find jump #3.

This chapter highlights the art form of handling your dog from the start line through the first few obstacles. What you do at the beginning of each run will dramatically influence your success on the sequence that follows.

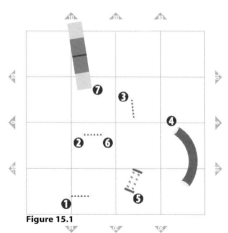

Figure 15.1

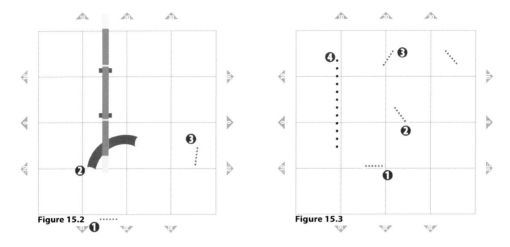

Figure 15.2

Figure 15.3

Prerequisite Skills

To handle your dog in an orderly fashion at the beginning of any run, he must have a solid *stay*. While this seems obvious, many handlers let their dog's *stay* deteriorate very quickly. Make sure to continually reinforce your dog's *stay* with the same enthusiasm you bring to the other aspects of agility. If you are having problems, see Chapter 24: Effective Problem-Solving Techniques.

Teaching Yourself to Handle Start Line Challenges
Step 1
The first step in handling a discrimination between two obstacles when it immediately follows the first obstacle is to consider where you will position your dog on his *sit-stay*. Your goal is to help your dog see the correct obstacle more clearly than he sees the incorrect obstacle. This generally means that you need to position him at an angle. If you consider the tunnel/dogwalk discrimination in Figure 15.2, he should be set at an angle directly looking at the tunnel.

Step 2
Your next step is to lead out but not so far that your dog can easily duck behind you and up the dogwalk. (See Photo 15.A.) As he clears the jump, drive the diagonal line as you learned before to push him into the tunnel. (See Photo 15.B.) Think of shoving on his bubble to get him in. Keep moving forward until your dog is committed to going into the tunnel. See Figure 15.4 for the correct positioning for this scenario. If you dart away too quickly, your pup will pull toward you and likely run up the dogwalk. Continue

> **Take Note**
> I often hear novice handlers talking in terms of blocking obstacles. In reality, you cannot block an obstacle if your dog really wants to take it. I have seen dogs run right between a handler's legs to get into a tunnel. It is more useful to think in terms of shaping your dog's path so that he takes the obstacles you want.

Intermediate Handling Skills

15.A: Lead out but not so far that your dog can easily duck behind you.
15.B: Drive the diagonal line to push your dog into the tunnel.

to face the tunnel and look at it until he vanishes.

Let's look at another configuration in Figure 15.5, which is slightly more complicated. Consider where you would position your dog and how you would communicate that you want the tunnel. It might first appear that you could start with your dog on your right and push him to the tunnel as you just did. You could do this, but it would leave you in an awkward position to pull your dog around and onto the dogwalk. It would also leave you in an awkward spot to pick him up to perform jump #4. It makes more sense to pull the dog toward the tunnel rather than pushing. This will get you in the correct position to wrap your dog onto the dogwalk after he exits the tunnel. With him on your left, you are also well positioned for jump #4.

To give your dog a fighting chance of executing this discrimination correctly:

1. Position him at a sharp angle facing the tunnel.
2. Position yourself well to the side of the tunnel and face him. (See Photo 15.C.)
3.

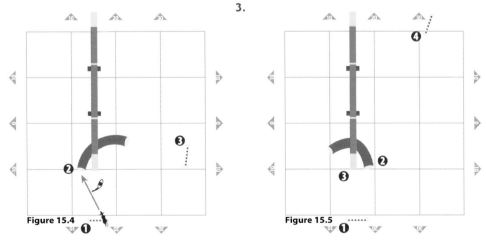

Figure 15.4

Figure 15.5

Getting Started on Course

15.C: Position yourself well to the side of the tunnel, and call your dog.
15.D: Once he is quite close to you, rotate toward the tunnel and send him in.

Release him and call him directly to you. Whenever you face your dog and call him, he should come on that line.

4. Once he is quite close to you, rotate toward the tunnel and send him in. (See Photo 15.D.)

This timing may take some practice. Make sure to keep your arms low so that you don't accidentally send him to the dogwalk. Figure 15.6 demonstrates the strategy to shape the dog's path.

On this kind of opening, you may be tempted to try facing the tunnel, calling your dog to your left hand and sending him into it. The problem is that once you turn your back, your dog sees both the dogwalk and the tunnel as attractive options. He will choose whichever one has the greater payoff in

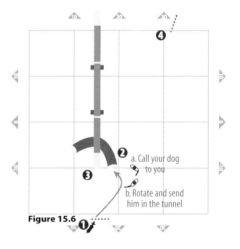

a. Call your dog to you
b. Rotate and send him in the tunnel

Figure 15.6

his mind. Although it takes a bit more time to call the dog toward you and then push him into the tunnel as described, this is definitely a more reliable method of handling this opening.

Teaching Tough Angles

You will undoubtedly find yourself faced with some challenging angles at the beginning of intermediate courses too. If you look at the opening in Figure 15.7, you can see that a dog set up facing jump #1 has no idea where he is going.

There are two skills that you can use to handle awkward angles efficiently. The first is to create a straight line between the first and second obstacles. On Figure 15.7, you can see that a dog set at an angle sees the first two obstacles as a simple straight line. You will often see handlers crouching behind the first jump like golfers looking at a putt. What they are doing is looking for the best line between the first obstacles so that they know where to leave their pup.

Intermediate Handling Skills

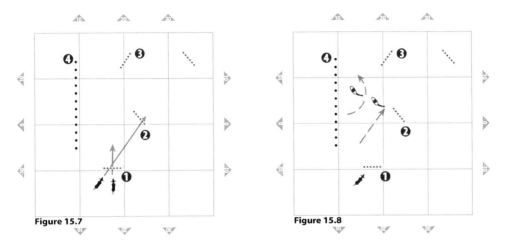

Figure 15.7

Figure 15.8

The second skill is to use your lateral distance. Consider the two handler strategies in Figure 15.8. As you can see, the handler who stays close to jump #2 pushes her dog past the jump and makes it difficult for him to find jump #3. The handler who sends her dog to jump #2 from a position off to the side is able to pull him around the corner with no problem. If you have worked lateral distance on course, you will find this process easy.

Step 1
Use the configuration in Figure 15.8. Bring your toy or big cookies out.
1. Position your dog on a straight line from jump #1 to jump #2.
2. Lead out and release him. Handle from the distance you would normally select.
3. As your dog takes the jump, toss your reinforcement from your left hand just beyond the spot where your dog lands after the second jump.
4. Repeat several times.

Step 2
Gradually migrate sideways. Remember to cue your dog with your arm to go forward. Continue to reinforce him for going to the second jump even though you are no longer as close. Play this game until you can cue him to travel forward while you position yourself close to the third jump.

Step 3
Handle the first two obstacles as you have been doing. This time, call your dog as soon as he commits to the second jump, and direct him over the third jump. You will have to experiment with the timing of your call. Call too early and responsive dogs may pull off the jump; call too late and he will waste strides driving forward. Work to create as tight a line as possible.

Step 4
Reverse the obstacles and practice the game going in the other direction.

Step 5

Create some awkward angles yourself with a few jumps. Continue to work your dog so that he understands how to "read" your lateral distance.

Using Other Skills

There are other skills you have learned that come into play at the beginning of sequences. Let's look at Figure 15.9, a replica of the first map in this chapter, to consider what successful handlers did to pull their dog around the corner to jump #3 with the A-frame looming large.

The three skills that worked here were lateral distance, strong shoulder pull, and change of speed. It was essential that handlers stayed well

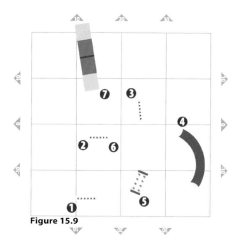

Figure 15.9

inside the curve rather than racing toward the second jump, which told the dogs to go straight ahead. The handlers also needed to turn their shoulder and feet as soon as the dog committed to jump #2. If they waited until the dog landed, they were lost to the contact. Most interesting, successful handlers used a speed change in two completely different ways. Some hesitated between jumps #2 and #3. This pulled the dog toward them and allowed them to direct him to the jump and the tunnel. This worked only if they were clearly facing to the right and not at the A-frame. Other handlers chose to accelerate between jumps #2 and #3, which got their dog's attention and pulled him to the tunnel.

Getting Started Issues

Habit and lack of attention to detail are your biggest enemies when it comes to handling the beginning of each course efficiently and correctly. It is easy to pay lots of attention to a course in general and to forget to strategize exactly how you will get started. Each time you run, your planning should include where you place your dog, where you will stand on your lead out, how you will orient your body, and what specific skills you will bring into play. Remember that each run will either begin smoothly, with you in control, or chaotically, with your dog guessing where to go.

Heel and Side

Make sure that your dog knows *heel* and *side* (heeling on the right) so that you can get him lined up exactly where you want behind the first obstacle without a wrestling match. Once you go into the ring, you shouldn't need to handle your dog other than to remove his leash.

Intermediate Handling Skills

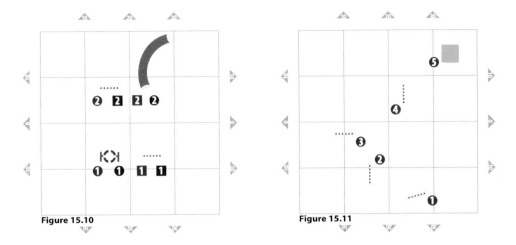

Figure 15.10   **Figure 15.11**

Mental Practice

You can practice setting up your dog correctly at the start line and handling discriminations with just a few obstacles. Consider how you would handle each of the following in Figure 15.10. Remember to consider what you want your dog to be looking at each time you put him on his *stay*.

You can make this game more challenging by substituting any of the obstacles with another that your dog loves. For example, if you substitute a table for jump #2, many dogs would want to go that way because they have earned a lot of cookies there. This will help you concentrate on your setup and handling so that you get him to take one of the other sequences.

Now let's try a longer sequence that is best handled by positioning your dog on the straight line between the first two jumps and utilizing lateral distance. (See Figure15.11.) What additional skill might you use?

Answer: Handlers who had good lateral distance were able to get far enough ahead that they could drive the line to the table. A few even front crossed nicely between jumps #3 and #4. Other handlers who stayed too close to their dogs had trouble making the turn to the table.

Concluding Thoughts

One thing that separates outstanding handlers from the pack is their attention to detail. They know exactly where they will leave their dog when they are preparing to run and precisely what movements they will make to direct their dog over the first sequence of obstacles. Make this a part of every walk-through that you do in class and at trials.

Practice setting up your dog correctly at the start line and handling discriminations with just a few obstacles.

Getting Started on Course

Part III
Preparing for Intermediate Sequences

As you have been learning new intermediate skills, our focus has been on short sequences that allow you to isolate and perfect the handling maneuver. As you grow comfortable with serpentines, false turns, and the other tools you've learned for communicating with your dog at the intermediate level, you will want to gradually integrate them into longer sequences. This section of the book is about how to prepare for long sequences so that your dog does them successfully and with confidence.

The next three chapters are attached at the hip. First, we will discuss the process for planning to run a longer sequence. Next, we will review how you can identify likely challenges for your dog. In the last chapter, we will review a powerful process for preparing your dog to handle those difficult sections successfully.

16
The Walk-Through

When you and your dog are practicing a few obstacles set in a simple pattern, you probably don't see the need for more than a glance at the sequence before you run. As soon as you progress to more than a few obstacles or add an intermediate skill to a sequence, such as direction changes, side changes, or discriminations between two obstacles, walking and planning become essential.

The walk-through is the process of looking at sequence obstacles methodically to maximize the chances of a mistake-free run. The walk-through is another place in agility where attention to detail pays off.

Six Walk-Through Steps
There are five stages that compose a walk-through at a trial. During a practice session or class, there is a very important sixth step.

Step 1: Observe Obstacle Flow
The first part of a walk-through should concentrate on the general flow of the obstacles. Where are the straight lines? When are the curves? Are there pinwheels?

Resist the urge during this phase to figure how you will handle, and focus on the general pattern before you settle down to details. I would suggest that you have completed this phase when you can close your eyes, and without peeking, say the obstacles in sequence at the speed you will run. In my classes, I ask intermediate students to do this often.

Don't Be Shy!
Some beginners are self-conscious about gesturing and talking out loud to their imaginary dog during the walk-through. It is not only acceptable to do this when walking, it is a fine idea to do a dress rehearsal of what you will do and say before you get your dog involved.

The walk-through is the process of looking at sequence obstacles methodically to maximize the chances of a mistake-free run.

Step 2: Understand Your Dog's Perspective

Next, walk the sequence looking at it from your dog's perspective. For example, does the course turn to the left when your dog is looking straight ahead at the most inviting tunnel that has ever been on an agility course?

As we discussed in Part II, novice and intermediate courses both have definitely become more challenging, with more places on course where the dogs need to discriminate between two obstacles placed closely together. To see what your dog sees, crouch down behind different obstacles and see what visual choices he will have.

Step 3: Strategize Your Handling Technique

Now you are ready to strategize in detail how you will handle your dog. Think about your position relative to each obstacle. Where will your feet be pointing? What will your arms do? Do you need to run all the way to a jump, or can you send your dog laterally? Decide where you need to cross and whether it is better to rear cross or front cross. In addition to your physical cues, decide exactly what words you will say. For example, will the word "here" be strong enough to pull your dog away from the tunnel, or will you need to use his name and your *come* command?

Once you have decided which skills to use, practice executing them correctly. For example, you know how to cue a serpentine by rotating your upper body back and switching hands. You know how to cue lateral distance by raising your arm off to the side. You have the tools to tell your dog what to do at every part of a sequence. Practice each skill exactly as you will want to do it with your dog.

In addition, consider your timing. As you walk your front cross, visualize yourself crossing before your dog takes off. Imagine exactly the moment you will change speeds to a sprint as you send him down a long line of jumps. Picture yourself driving the line at exactly the right moment to get him into a tunnel or onto the table.

Preparing for Intermediate Sequences

Step 4: Run Your Invisible Dog

Frequently, people do a thorough walk-through but then get thrown off plan when they shift from walking to running with their dog. Commonly, folks will look down at their dogs and then look up and find themselves disoriented. To prevent this, end your walk-through by running your invisible dog to see how things look with some speed. Use your verbal commands and body language as you have planned. Look down and then back up exactly as you will do it. Practice the sequence exactly as you will run it.

Take Note

Your dog is quite busy when he is doing agility. Chatting at him is not helpful, and it is often a distraction. Use as few words as possible as verbal cues while he runs, and make sure that your words make sense. I occasionally hear handlers say something such as "Here go over." The dog has no idea whether to come toward the handler or run ahead. Most dogs learn to handle conflicting information by simply ignoring us, which does not lead to a good result in agility.

Step 5: Visualize Your Run

Your dress rehearsal does not need to end when your walk-through is over. All top athletes use the power of visualization. Any time you are waiting, continue to picture exactly how you will run your dog. Mental practice is often as good as more walking. We will discuss this in Chapter 25, when we talk about course memorization.

Step 6: Identify the Challenging Sections

If you are walking a sequence during a class or practice session, there is one more essential step: Identify the sections that will be tough for your dog. Falling back on the thought *I'll just see how he does* is rarely a good idea.

To pull this off, isolate and pre-practice those sections where your dog might make an error. In Chapter 17, we will talk about how you can locate potential challenges on a course.

Concluding Thoughts

I find it difficult to convince students that they should devote this much energy to planning for each sequence. It is easier to just get through a class sequence and then go back and try to get it right. This is not a good idea for two reasons. First, once a dog does something "wrong," it puts that idea in his mind. It takes multiple repetitions of the correct behavior to wipe out that mistake. It is almost always better in dog training to help your dog get something right the first time than make mistakes and loop back to try to fix them. Second, there are no second chances at trials. Making a habit of doing and then redoing creates a casual mindset that will hurt later if you want to compete.

This is not to say that you should despair if your dog makes mistakes. Everyone makes mistakes in training and trialing. However, your training goal should be to handle longer sequences so that the odds are very high that your dog will get it right.

17 Identifying the Challenges

To help your dog nail more challenging sequences, it is ideal to identify the parts that may be difficult for him before you run. With that information in hand, you can do some training to make sure that he is prepared to get it right.

The challenges that you will encounter on course come in two types. Some are individual, and some are difficult for almost every dog initially.

Individual Challenges

At some point during their training, virtually every dog encounters something that baffles or worries him. For example, a Miniature Pinscher in one of my classes worried about dark tunnels for weeks after the other dogs were blasting though. As a result, we gave her a chance to practice each tunnel before we put it in a sequence. We shortened the tunnel if necessary to build her confidence. Gradually, she grew to love tunnels of every shape, and now she flies through as well as anyone.

Your dog may want to skip an occasional jump or worry about the dogwalk. He may struggle with reading the front cross so that he doesn't always turn as tightly as he could. He may sometimes forget his contact performance if he is running really fast. He may not read your cue for the rear cross and may spin the wrong way.

Your partner can overcome any of these issues with a little extra attention. It bears repeating that allowing a dog to try something too difficult and fail is never a good training plan.

Common Challenges

Agility challenges can be clustered into categories. These will sound familiar. The intermediate skills you have been learning have been developed to address these:

- changes of direction
- consistent contact performance
- discriminations between two or more obstacles
- getting the correct end of the tunnel
- long straight lines
- obstacles set at unusual angles
- obstacles that must be handled at a distance
- running past other obstacles to get to the correct obstacle
- serpentines with jumps and other obstacles
- tough weave pole entries
- wide turns (such as a 180 or 270)

> **Take Note**
> Naturally, unexpected things happen in agility because it is a complex activity. But you shouldn't launch off on course if you are not confident that you and your dog are able to deliver a fast, precise performance.

Although you could probably come up with others on a long winter night, these capture the majority of intermediate challenges.

Mental Practice

Let's take a look at a few sequences. On Figures 17.1, 17.2, and 17.3, practice identifying the intermediate challenge(s). Can you determine the types of challenges presented in each?

Challenge #1

The first challenge in Figure 17.1 is the change of direction at jump #5. Practicing your front cross, in which you wrap your dog tightly around the stanchion, will help him travel an efficient path. The second tough spot is the tunnel/A-frame discrimination. This is a classic spot to use your skill of driving the line. Your dog's chance of correctly getting the whole sequence will be greatly increased by practicing these two skills separately and then together before trying the whole sequence.

Challenge #2

The first challenge in the sequence in Figure 17.2 is the 270-degree turn from jump #5 to jump #6. This wide turn is made more difficult by the placement of the teeter, which the dog will see as he travels from jump to jump. The second challenge, the line from jump #7 to the table, may present an individual difficulty. For any dog who drives ahead of the handler, he will come face to face

> **Inherent Breed Behaviors**
> Although every dog is different, it is helpful to remember that groups of dogs tend toward certain behaviors that may provide challenges. For example, some herding breeds have a tendency to curve back toward their handler. Terriers find it hard to ignore a gopher kicking dirt on the perimeter of the field. As with the other challenges mentioned in this chapter, you can work through most issues with enough patience and positive reinforcement.

Preparing for Intermediate Sequences

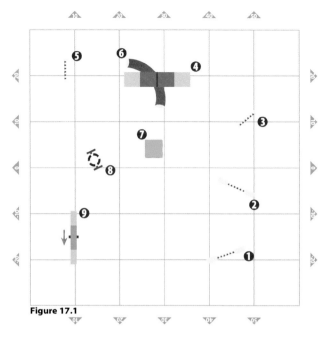

Figure 17.1

with the poles rather than the table. With this type of dog, the handler must stay well to the left of jump #7 to pull him in that direction.

Challenge #3

The intermediate challenge in Figure 17.3 is the tunnel #6 entry. For a dog approaching at full speed, either entry could be correct. This section deserves a bit of advanced practice as you put your false turn maneuver into action. The broad jump is an obstacle that may present an individual challenge because inexperienced dogs often don't perceive it as a jump.

Concluding Thoughts

If you subscribe to an agility magazine or have saved old maps from trials, pull those out. Judges are required to build certain challenges into each course they design. Identify the tough spots you find in each intermediate course. This practice will help you find potential problems quickly so that you can make a handling plan and a training plan.

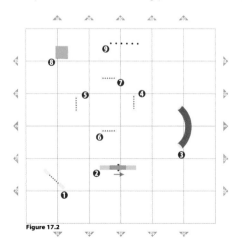

Figure 17.2

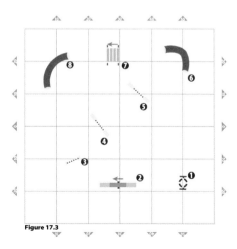

Figure 17.3

Identifying the Challenges

147

18

The Power of Backchaining

During your life, you have probably had one great teacher who taught you new things in a way that made you feel confident and capable. One thing these teachers do is to make sure that their students have the skills they need before they launch into a project. They preteach vocabulary, drill students on discrete math skills, and explain essential concepts. They never hand out a complex assignment while muttering *Ah, let's see what happens.*

Good agility trainers are outstanding teachers. They follow the same policy of making sure that their canine partner is ready to handle what he will encounter on course. In this chapter, we are going to focus on a training method that is immensely powerful for teaching your dog what is coming: backchaining. It is my favorite training method in all of agility because it practically guarantees that the dog will be successful.

What Is Backchaining?

Backchaining is the process of teaching the end of a sequence first and then working your way backward. Its power lies in the fact that the dog always knows what to do next and can drive forward with confidence and speed. You may choose to backchain an entire sequence or just the section that offers a challenge.

Let's take a look at Figure 18.1 and discuss how you would use the process of backchaining. This pinwheel is hard because of the draw of the A-frame, which lies straight ahead of jump #1. Most dogs will choose the contact equipment because they have been reinforced with many cookies there. By backchaining this sequence, you will reinforce your dog for not taking the A-frame until the correct time after jump #5.

Backchaining is the process of teaching the end of a sequence first and then working your way backward.

1. Start by sending your dog over jump #4 first. (Starting with jump #5 might send him over the A-frame.) Reinforce jump #4 with a cookie or game of tug.
2. Next send your dog over jumps #3 and #4. Reinforce.
3. Then send your pup over jumps #2, #3, and #4. Reinforce.
4. Now add jump #1. Make sure to start your dog at a sharp angle so that he is facing jump #2. Given the draw of the A-frame, you might toss a large cookie onto the ground close to the second jump after he clears the first one. This will tell him what path you want him to take.
5. Next return him to jump #1 and ask him to do the entire pinwheel. Make sure to angle your start. This time, add jump #5 and drive to the A-frame. Adding the last two obstacles will be easy for your dog once he nails the pinwheel.

Backchaining works on every combination of obstacles. Because the dog always knows what he is doing next, it encourages him to look for the next obstacle rather than look back at you. As you know, excessive focus on you is not good because it slows down the dog and sometimes causes him to miss obstacles.

A second benefit of backchaining is that the process allows you to focus on perfect performance on each obstacle. When you start each sequence at the beginning, there is a tendency to continue moving forward even if the dog's performance is less than ideal. When you are backchaining, you can stop and work on any individual obstacle if you encounter a behavior that is not what you want.

You might think that this process would bore a dog because he has to repeat parts of the sequence several times. This is rarely true. Dogs enjoy repetition of games in which they know what is expected and when they are generously reinforced for doing it well.

Preparing for Intermediate Sequences

Backchaining Obstacle by Obstacle

When your dog is still relatively inexperienced, it is best to work backward obstacle by obstacle. In the next section, we will talk about backchaining groups of obstacles.

Let's practice on a sequence in Figure 18.2 that includes a different contact obstacle. The sequence is more difficult than it might seem at first. The dog must demonstrate considerable self-control to hold his dogwalk contact when traveling at high speed.

1. Start with the dogwalk.
2. Work your way back obstacle by obstacle to the tire.
3. By the time you are ready to start at the tire, your dog will be driving ahead of you confidently.
4. If at any time your dog is unable to do his contact in the way you want, shorten the sequence and reinforce generously when he gets it right.

There is one danger with this game. Smart dogs who get rewarded only at the end (on the dogwalk in this case) will start to think that they may as well go directly to that obstacle. You can keep this from happening by surprising your pup with his toy or a cookie somewhere other than the dogwalk. For example, one time toss his tug or a chunk of cheese after he takes jump #3 or when he comes out of the tunnel. Then rev him up and head off for the next obstacle.

Let's look at Figure 18.3 and do one more practice sequence, this one with the teeter. The teeter is placed purposefully at the beginning so that the dog doesn't approach it at too much speed and scare

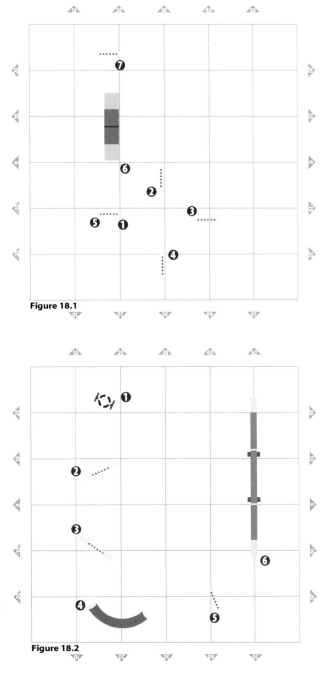

Figure 18.1

Figure 18.2

The Power of Backchaining

himself. This sequence provides you with an opportunity to practice leaving your dog on the table to get in position to front cross between jumps #3 and #5. Start by sending your dog over jump #7 and then work your way backward obstacle by obstacle.

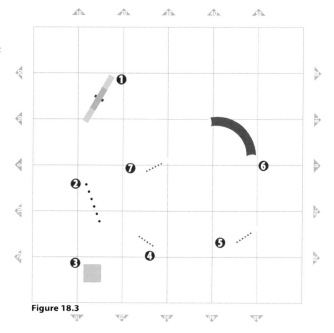

Figure 18.3

Backchaining Clusters of Obstacles

As your dog becomes more experienced and you tackle longer sequences, you can accelerate this game by backchaining clusters of obstacles. Let's look at Figure 18.4, featuring a sequence from the previous chapter. There are no absolute rules about the order of backchaining. I will suggest one way to practice this sequence. See if you would do it the same way or differently.

1. Have your dog perform obstacles #8 and #9 first, which will allow him to focus on the weave entry.
2. Then practice obstacles #4 to #7, which highlight the 270-degree turn.
3. Finish by letting your dog do obstacles #1 to #3, which will prepare him for the teeter.
4. During this process, it is also fine if you include an obstacle twice. For example, you might do tunnel #3 as part of the opening and then as part of the box that follows.
5. Once your dog understands each section, try the whole sequence.

How would you split up the sequence in Figure 18.5 for backchaining?

The two tricky parts are the pull to the table and the pull to get the dog into the chute. It would make sense to split these challenges into different sections. Again, there is no hard and fast rule,

Balancing Handler and Obstacle Focus

Agility requires a balance of obstacle focus and handler focus from your dog. That is, he should actively look for the next obstacle while reacting to your handling cues. If a dog has an excess of either type of focus, he will struggle with agility. Most dogs are inherently interested in their human partner. The process of backchaining will help him build an equal balance of obstacle focus.

Preparing for Intermediate Sequences

but it would work to group the obstacles like this: #10 to #12, #6 to #9, #1 to #6. You might even do obstacles #6 to #12 before you practice the final group. Then put the whole thing together and watch your dog ace it.

> **Take Note**
> Remember that to backchain any sequence, your dog must already know how to perform the individual obstacles in the sequence at the level you will want in competition.

Concluding Thoughts

Recently I worked with a friend who has a lively young dog who is naturally fast but had developed a habit of looking at his handler before performing each obstacle. This caused him to miss many obstacles because he didn't see what was coming. We began to backchain every sequence to build his confidence and obstacle focus. He loved the system because he knew exactly where he was going. He began to understand that his handler's body language would tell him what to do even if he kept running. This investment paid off with a dog who now has terrific speed and the confidence to drive way ahead of his handler to find the next obstacle.

In upcoming chapters, we will be looking at a variety of longer sequences in which you will have a chance to apply your understanding of all of the skills in Parts II and III, including backchaining.

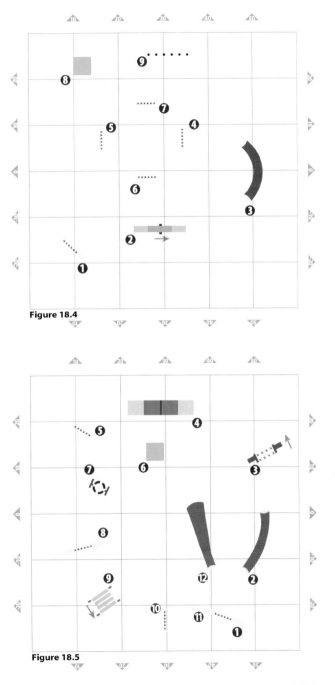

Figure 18.4

Figure 18.5

The Power of Backchaining

Part IV
On Course

In this section, you will find exercises to keep you and your dog busy for months. The first chapter will present shorter sequences that focus on two to four skills. It will be divided into two sections:

- exercises without contact equipment, which you can set up with jumps, tunnels, weaves, and tables
- exercises that include contact equipment

The second chapter will provide you with intermediate courses that include two or more of the skills you have been learning. Make sure that you take time to identify the sections that will be challenging for your dog, and backchain these before you tackle the whole sequence.

In both chapters, I will highlight the primary skills that you should use for each exercise.

Where there is an alternative method to handle a sequence, I will suggest that you try that. You may want to try different strategies even if they are not as comfortable for you. This will expand your range of skills.

I will also suggest opportunities to backchain parts of a sequence when they include new or challenging skills. However, it is up to you to know your dog and practice any sections that he will find difficult. For example, never be shy about taking your dog and a toy out on course to remind him how to do a 270-degree turn before you encounter it in a sequence. Never hesitate to take him out and show him the teeter before he hits it at speed. Even with very experienced dogs, my teacher recommends that we go out and work through difficult sections before we run long sequences. As a result, dogs will run with confidence and make fewer mistakes that need to be fixed.

Remember that if you are practicing on your own, always stop an exercise while your dog is enthusiastic and would like to go on. If he has trouble with an exercise, stop for the day. Take some time to figure out how to help him understand, and give it a try the next day.

I n the earlier chapters, there are, of course, many sequences that be can set up to perfect your skills. This chapter contains additional practice opportunities. If you don't have a tire, you can always substitute another jump. You may also substitute jumps without wings, although the wings generally increase the difficulty a bit.

Sequences Without Contacts

These sequences are for those of you who have acquired the smaller equipment but have not yet purchased the costly contact equipment. These will keep you busy until you give in and order that A-frame or dogwalk.

Sequence 1

Figure 19.1 is a straightforward exercise with two options:

- **Front cross:** Execute your cross between jump #3 and the tunnel. See how tightly you can pull your dog around the corner.
- **Rear cross:** Now try

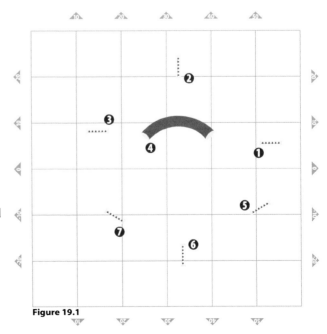

Figure 19.1

pulling your dog into the tunnel after the jump, and rear cross after he is safely in the tunnel. Check out which strategy is faster.

As long as your dog is confident performing jumps set on simple arcs like you see here, there is no need to use backchaining on this sequence.

Sequence 2

The exercise in Figure 19.2 puts three skills into action:

- **Handling the opening:** Lead out so that you will be even with your dog's head as he clears the tire.
- **Driving the line:** Run a clear path to jump #3 so that he doesn't race into the tunnel after the tire.

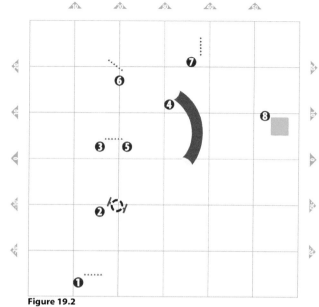

Figure 19.2

Wings generally increase the difficulty of a jump.

- **Shoulder pull:** As soon as your dog commits to jump #3, strongly turn your shoulders and feet to cue tunnel #4.

You may want to backchain obstacles #1 to #3, starting at jump #3. This helps show the dog that the tunnel is not the correct obstacle after the tire, and it has the added benefit of working the tire, which is often tough for dogs.

Sequence 3

As soon as you look at the sequence in Figure 19.3, the serpentine formed by obstacles #5 to #7 should leap out at you. You will use two skills in completing this sequence:

- **Serpentine:** Handle this classic serpentine entirely with your dog on your left. Remember to use your upper body rotation to cue jump #6.
- **Shoulder pull:** The turn from the tire to the table is a bit tricky because of the dummy jump. Use a strong shoulder pull to get your dog to the table. As an alternative strategy, you could front cross between the tire and the table.

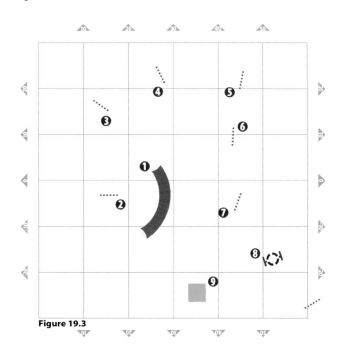

Figure 19.3

I recommend that you take your dog out and practice the three-jump serpentine before running the whole sequence. Then backchain by running obstacles #4 to #7 and #3 to #7. If that goes well, you are cleared for the whole sequence.

Sequence 4

The exercise in Figure 19.4 highlights how moving one obstacle dramatically changes your handling. As you can see, the sequence is identical to the previous one through the serpentine, but now the table has moved. The skills you will need are:

- **Front cross:** Cross between jumps #5 and #6. This will put you in the correct position after the serpentine to pull your dog back to jump #7 and then to the table.
- **Weave pole entry:** The line from jump #9 to the weaves could easily send your dog into the poles incorrectly unless he knows his entry. Put on entry wires to practice and then try it without.

Multi-Skill Practice Sequences

This course calls for backchaining on two sections. Practice jumps #4 to #7. Work on a timely front cross to get a very tight path on the serpentine. Then practice the section from the table through the weaves. Starting with the poles will help your dog get that right.

Sequence 5

The sequence in Figure 19.5 highlights two skills:

- **Speed changes:** Accelerate from obstacles #1 to #4. Decelerate before jump #5 to cue the change of direction
- **Front cross:** Cross between jump #5 and tunnel #6.

As long as your dog is comfortable handling a straightforward line of jumps as presented in this exercise, there is no need to backchain. But remember to dramatically change your body language when you accelerate and decelerate.

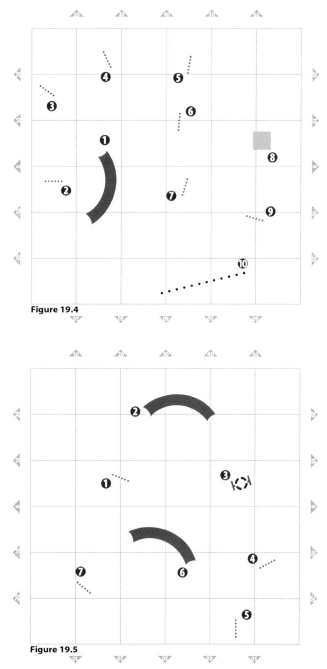

Figure 19.4

Figure 19.5

Take Note
Always make a clear plan for what you are teaching your dog. You can get by with less training than you think if it is carefully thought out. Before you take your dog out to the field, think about what skills you want to teach him and exactly how you are going to set him up for success.

160

On Course

Sequence 6

This exercise in Figure 19.6 looks quite simple but requires three skills:

- **Handling the opening:** Make sure that you handle jumps #2 and #3 laterally so that your dog does not go into the tunnel.

- **180-degree turn:** The two winged jumps form a classic 180-degree turn. Rotate your shoulder to help your dog find the second jump.

- **Driving the line:** After jump #7, the dog is on a line to take the wrong end of the tunnel. You can prevent this by getting ahead of your dog when he is in tunnel #6. As he clears jump #7, pick up his head and drive hard toward the correct end of the tunnel.

The sequence lends itself to backchaining three sections: obstacles #1 to #4, #3 to #6, and #6 to #8. The overlaps will help your dog transition between sections when you run the whole thing.

Sequence 7

The exercise in Figure 19.7 is similar to the last one except that the angle of jump #7 is changed, as is the end of tunnel #8. Again, your dog is headed for an off course in two places without careful handling. Use these skills:

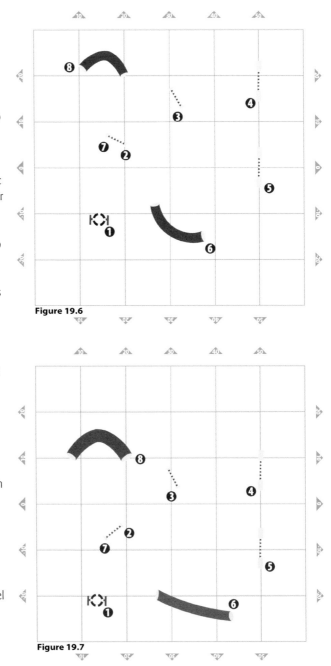

Figure 19.6

Figure 19.7

- **Handling the opening:** This exercise presents an interesting challenge right off the bat. As the dog rounds the corner from jump #2 to jump #3, he is looking right at the #8 tunnel, which is not the correct obstacle. To get him around this corner without an off course, handle laterally and pull hard to jump #3. If necessary, use your dog's name for extra emphasis.
- **180-degree turn:** Rotate your shoulders to help your dog around this turn at jumps #4 and #5.
- **False turn:** Use this maneuver to pull your dog toward you. When you have his attention, rotate back and send him into the correct end of the tunnel.

You can help your dog by backchaining at least two segments of this sequence. Work on jumps #1 to #3 and obstacles #6 to #8. If you did the previous exercise, you may not need to isolate the 180-degree turn.

Sequence 8

Figure 19.8 is a segment from a course that has a discrimination that took many intermediate handlers by surprise. Most folks started the sequence with their dog on their left. They led out about halfway to the tire and as their dog approached, they veered toward the tire and called their dogs rather casually. Many saw their dogs vanish into the tunnel. This discrimination requires a much stronger effort, so try these skills:

- **Handling the opening:** The most successful strategy was to lead out close to the tire and well off to the side. This positioning and the lateral distance worked to pull most dogs to the tire. A few handlers added a quick false turn to pull the dog in. As an alternative, try leading out and driving the line from jump #2 to the tire. This works best with dogs who don't drive too far ahead.
- **Rear cross:** Cross at jump #4 to turn the dog around the corner. Rear cross again at jump #8.

It is well worth your time to backchain obstacles #1 to #3. You may also want to practice sections #4 to #6 and #7 to #9 to review the rear cross.

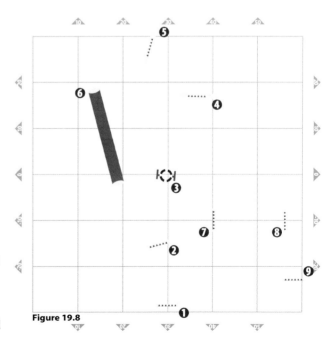

Figure 19.8

Sequence 9

The sequence in Figure 19.9 is taken from an intermediate-level course. As you can see, the challenges start right away. Use these skills:

- **Handling the opening:** Lead

out just past the weaves. Call your dog directly to you and then push him into the poles on your left hand.

- **270-degree turn:** To help your dog maintain his arc around the wide turn between jumps #5 and #6, stay right across from his head and move as far into the gap between the two jumps as he needs.

Backchain the first three obstacles. Put the weave pole guide wires on the entry if needed to help your dog get it right. Then preview obstacles #4 to #6 to reinforce the big turn.

Sequence 10

The setup in Figure 19.10 lends itself to dozens of different exercises. After you finish this exercise, create your own sequence. Use these skills:

- **Speed changes:** Go full speed ahead through this exercise except at jumps #5 and #11, where you should decelerate to cue the changes of direction.
- **Front cross:** Cross between jumps #5 and #6 and then between jumps #11 and #12.

To backchain this sequence, start with obstacles #1 to #6. Focus on the correct timing for your front cross. Then backchain the second half of the course. Again, concentrate on the timing

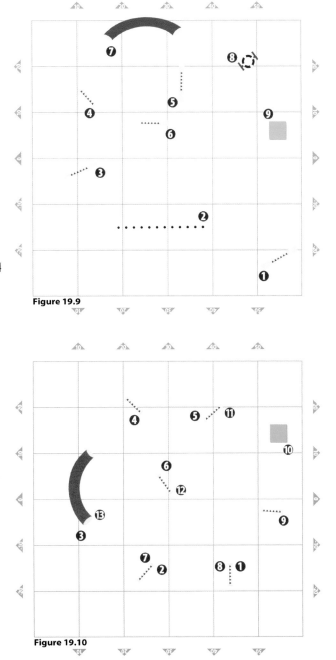

Figure 19.9

Figure 19.10

Multi-Skill Practice Sequences

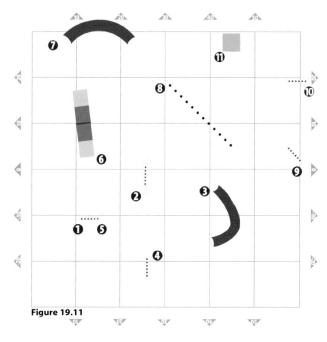

Figure 19.11

of your front cross between jumps #11 and #12 so that your dog knows exactly where he is going. Finish by putting the whole sequence together.

Sequences With Contacts

Because competition agility courses include contact obstacles, it is important that you sometimes include these in your practice sessions.

Sequence 11

The sequence in Figure 19.11 provides an opportunity to practice multiple skills. Pay special attention to:

• **Handling the opening:** Leave your dog at the start line. (Angle sharply toward jump #2.) Face your feet and shoulders toward jump #2.

• **Lateral distance:** Work off to the side to pull your dog toward tunnel #3.

• **Front cross:** Hustle out between tunnel #7 and the weave poles to front cross to handle the weaves on your right. This puts you in the best position to pull your dog around the corner to the final obstacles. As an alternative, you could handle the weaves with your dog on your left and front cross at the end of the poles. Use guides on the last few poles if necessary to help your dog complete them while you rotate.

Backchain obstacles #1 to #4. Also backchain tunnel #7 to the weave poles because locating the weaves after the dark tunnel is often a challenge for less experienced dogs. If you plan to front cross at the end of the weaves, try that in advance. Otherwise, give this sequence a go.

Sequence 12

In addition to handling the contact obstacle, there are three primary skills involved in handling the intermediate sequence in Figure 19.12:

• **Discrimination:** Help your dog find the dogwalk by using the skills practiced earlier. These include using your dog's name, deceleration, and lateral distance. Make sure that you are consistent with your communication.

• **Front cross:** Cross between tire #7 and jump #8.

• **Speed changes:** Decelerate again to cue the front cross at the tire. Accelerate dramatically from obstacles #9 to #13.

On Course

You can also try rear crossing tunnel #9.

Backchain obstacles #3 to #5. Be aware that the tunnel will add significant speed, which makes the corner more challenging. If necessary, use a gate across the tunnel to help your dog find the dogwalk the first time. If he is getting confident from working through all of the previous exercises, try the rest without practicing first.

Sequence 13

The sequence in Figure 19.13 looks deceptively simple, but there are two distinct off-course possibilities. Both tunnels threaten to pull the dog into the wrong end. Put the following skills into action:

- **Shoulder pull:** As your dog does his A-frame contact, position yourself to pull toward jump #3 to avoid the dummy jump.
- **Lateral distance:** Rounding the corner from jumps #5 to #6, stay lateral so that you don't push your dog into the exit end of tunnel #8.
- **Rear cross:** Cross before jump #6. As an alternative, execute a front cross between jumps #5 and #6.
- **Driving the line:** Push your dog on a hard angle after the second A-frame to help him find tunnel #13.

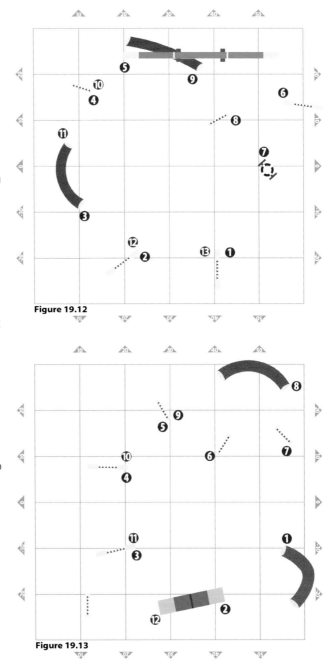

Figure 19.12

Figure 19.13

Multi-Skill Practice Sequences

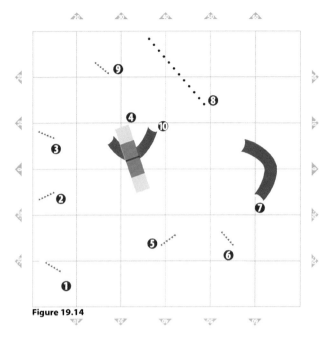

Figure 19.14

If your dog has done well on exercises to this point, try this exercise without backchaining. Make sure to ask for and reinforce exactly the A-frame performance you want on each pass at the obstacle.

Sequence 14

The sequence in Figure 19.14 provides the most challenging discrimination yet because the dog must choose the contact over two visible tunnel entries. Use these skills:

• **Discrimination:** Pull your dog to the A-frame on your left. Keep your eyes on him and the obstacle until he loads on.

• **Front cross:** While he holds his A-frame contact, front cross.

• **Weave pole entry:** Although this entry looks straightforward, the dog's speed from the tunnel and the slight angle deserves your attention.

• **Front cross:** Cross after jump #9. Remember to strongly decelerate to cue the cross so that your dog doesn't carry out too far.

• **Drive the line:** Pick up your dog's head and drive strongly at the #10 tunnel.

You can also rear cross jump #5.

Backchain obstacles #1 to #4. If your dog makes an error on the A-frame/tunnel discrimination, use gates to block the tunnel once or twice. Consider whether you need to backchain obstacles #5 to #10. Your decision should be based on your dog's skill in finding the weaves from a tunnel and whether you need to practice your timing on the front cross.

Sequence 15

The sequence in Figure 19.15 encourages you to combine two skills that you know, the serpentine and a front cross:

• **Serpentine:** Handle the three-jump serpentine all from the inside.

• **Front cross:** After you send your dog over jump #6, your best option is a cross before the teeter.

• **False turn:** Use this strategy to help your dog find the tunnel #11 entry.

You can also front cross the end of the teeter.

If your dog is handling weave pole entries well, skip right to backchaining the serpentine and front cross to the teeter (#4 to #7). If you try front crossing at the end of the teeter, make sure to practice that maneuver too so that your dog isn't startled.

Concluding Thoughts

With any collection of obstacles, you can create an endless array of practice sequences. If you have a good imagination, design a sequence once you decide what your dog needs to work on that day. If you are not good at laying out sequences, there are books and magazines that provide hundreds of design possibilities from short, focused exercises to long, multi-skill sequences.

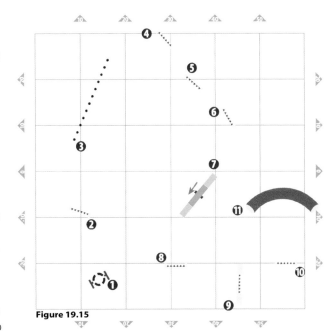

Figure 19.15

Obstacle Inclusion
Remember that you should include only obstacles in sequences that your dog can perform at the highest level. For example, if he is relearning his contact performance on the A-frame, don't include that obstacle in a sequence. Work on the A-frame by itself. Once he has mastered the exact behavior you want, then you can include that obstacle in a longer run.

20

Intermediate Courses

I n this chapter, there are five intermediate courses that I selected from real trials. This is a chance to practice all of the things we have discussed. Memorize the course and plan your run, complete with all of your handling moves and verbal cues. If you don't have access to an agility field, close your eyes and visualize running each course in detail. If you have a place to set it up, give each a try.

Five Intermediate Courses

The first three courses have limited options about how to handle them. I will suggest the best plan with minor alternative strategies. The last two are more difficult, and I will suggest different approaches for handling certain sections.

On these courses, I will not tell you to backchain this section or that section directly. However, each of the bullets highlights a section of the course that requires a specific skill. Unless you are sure that your dog will be successful, preview each of those parts of the course with your dog. If he needs more support to run with speed and precision, break the entire course into sections and take your time to teach him what is coming. In the long run, this will have a big payoff in terms of your dog's confidence.

Course 1

Figure 20.1 contains a fast course with three specific challenges: a discrimination, a serpentine, and a high-speed approach to the weave poles. Accelerate wherever you can. Consider the following strategies:
- Lead out as far down the tunnel as you can to avoid getting too far behind. It's great if you can get past the tunnel and call your dog through.
- Use your discrimination skills to get to the dogwalk.

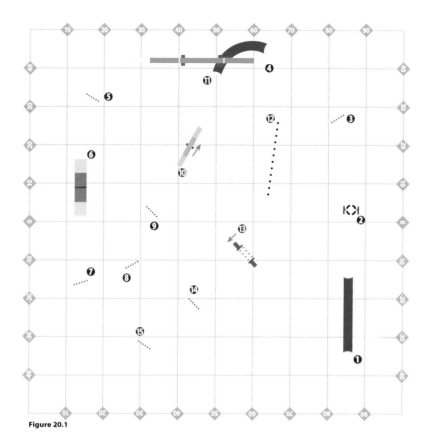

Figure 20.1

- Handle jumps #7 to #9 as a serpentine. If you handle from the left side, rear cross when you get to the tunnel. If you front cross after jump #7, no cross is needed.
- Decelerate between the tunnel and the weave poles to help your dog slow down enough to find the entry.

Course 2

Figure 20.2 presents a lovely course with nice flow and multiple opportunities to practice your front cross. Consider the following strategies:

- The first four obstacles can be handled on either side. However, starting with the dog on the right eliminates the rear cross at tunnel #4.
- Front cross after tunnel #4 to pull him onto the dogwalk.
- Front cross between tunnel #6 and jump #7.
- Front cross between the weaves and the teeter. Be careful about your timing so that you don't

On Course

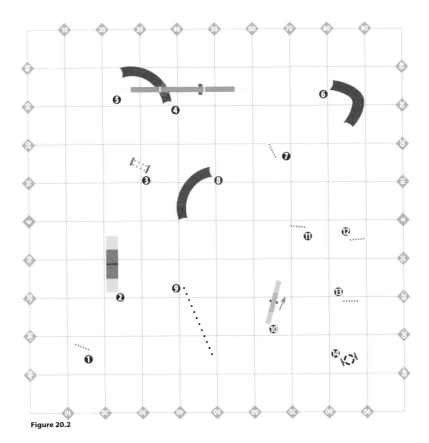

Figure 20.2

pull your dog out of the weave poles. An alternative here is to use a shoulder pull to the teeter and front cross at the end of the teeter. This is a riskier move in general.
- Use your 180-degree handling from jumps #11 to #12.
- Accelerate strongly through the closing line of obstacles.

Course 3

Figure 20.3 is another open course with appropriate intermediate challenges. Consider the following strategies:
- Lead out to the tire but not beyond. Release your dog to come to your right side.
- Start telling your dog that the weaves are coming right away. He will be excited coming off the start line, and there is a big danger that he will run past the entry. Slow down until he finds the entry.
- Use your discrimination skills to get the A-frame.

171

Intermediate Courses

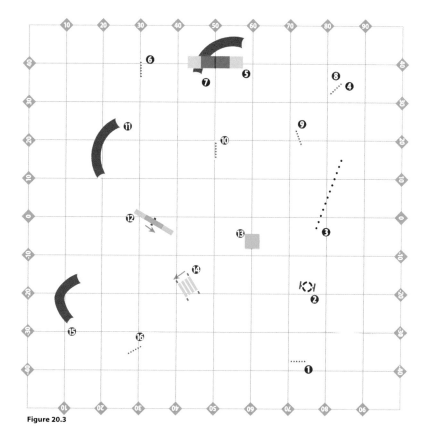

Figure 20.3

- Send your dog forward to jump #6. Front cross to pull him back. Make your cross very wide to get a good line to the tunnel and prevent him from going back up the A-frame
- Drive the line to the tunnel #7 entry.
- As you run the line from jump #8 to the #11 tunnel, you have two clear options. Try front crossing between jumps #9 and #10. This strategy will work well only if you can send your dog out to jump #8 and give yourself room and time to cross. If you need to run close to jump #8, keep the dog on your left and rear cross the tunnel.
- Take your dog off the table on your left and drive the line to the tunnel.
- You can either pull him to the final jump or front cross after the tunnel to pick him up on your right.

Handle Every Obstacle

As sequences get longer and longer, handlers have a tendency to get in a hurry. Rushing along and thinking too far ahead leads to mistakes on individual obstacles. Remember the agility mantra: Handle every obstacle.

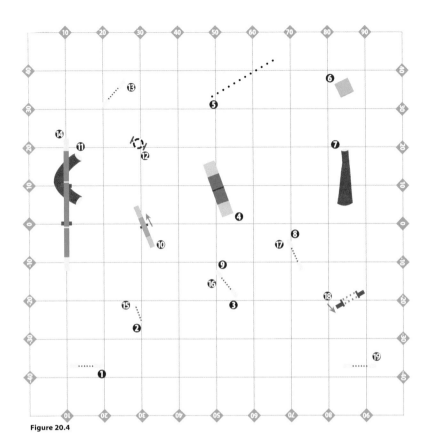

Figure 20.4

Course 4

The course in Figure 20.4 offers greater challenges. Consider the following strategies:

- The first four obstacles are set at angles that warrant your attention. One approach is to lead out just past jump #2. This will allow you to push your dog over jump #3 and shoulder pull to the A-frame. A second approach requires a great *stay*. You will lead out as close to jump #3 as possible. As your dog approaches, move forward (keeping your eyes on him) and front cross between jump #3 and the A-frame. This will leave you in a perfect position to cue the weave poles.
- If you complete the A-frame with your dog on your right, front cross at the bottom of that obstacle.
- Obstacles #9 to #11 up the ante. You have two choices to help your dog find the teeter. Use a strong shoulder pull between jump #9 and the teeter. You may need to add your dog's name. If you can get ahead of him, you have room to front cross between the jump and the teeter.
- If your dog is on your left at the end of the teeter, front cross right there and drive the line

Intermediate Courses

Intermediate courses can be tricky—you must pay attention to every obstacle and communicate clearly with your dog.

to the tunnel. If you front crossed before the teeter, you are already in the perfect position to drive the line.
- While your dog is in the tunnel, front cross and pick him up on your right hand after he exits. From there, use your shoulder pull to help him perform the arc of obstacles formed by the tire, jump #13, and the dogwalk.
- Once your dog performs the dogwalk, beware of moving away too quickly before he is firmly on the contact.
- The final series of jumps requires only a rear cross at jump #17.

Course 5

Figure 20.5 is a tough little course that I ran with a young dog. It required that the handler pay close attention virtually every step of the way. Try the following strategies:
- Lead out quite close to the poles. Call your dog to you, rotate, and push him into the poles.
- Drive the line to the teeter.
- Handle the serpentine by front crossing between jumps #4 and #5.
- There are two strategies to get the #10 tunnel. Try a front cross and drive the line to the tunnel. Then try a rear cross at jump #9. This will wrap your dog around the right stanchion. The rear cross is safer because it puts the dog on a straighter line to the tunnel.

> **Take Note**
> There is a significant leap in difficulty from novice-level courses to intermediate-level courses. Be patient with yourself and your dog as you learn to string together all of the skills you have learned.

On Course

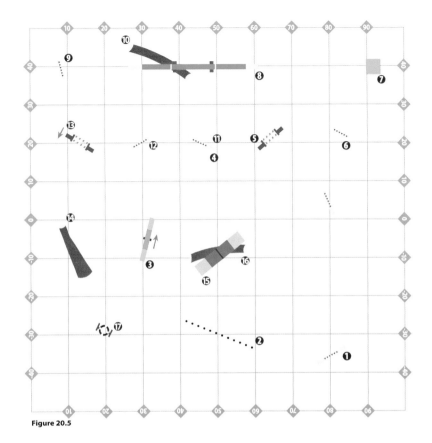
Figure 20.5

- Handle the second serpentine by front crossing after jump #11.
- Front cross between the chute and the A-frame. This is very tight, so keep your eyes on your dog.
- Front cross the bottom of the A-frame to pull your dog into the tunnel.
- Drive the line to the tire to finish.

Concluding Thoughts

As you can see, intermediate courses get very tricky. They require that you pay attention to every obstacle and use your communication system consistently so that your dog knows what you want. I often tell students to think of "fighting for every obstacle." Any moment of casual handling will cause your dog to go off course or miss an obstacle. When you make mistakes on courses, file away the information for short, focused practice sessions at home.

Part V

Solving Common Intermediate-Level Problems

Agility is a wonderfully complex sport—and this is what keeps it interesting. However, complexity also leaves lots of room for human errors as we work with our canine partners. The first three chapters in this section discuss three common problems that arise in agility as a result of our interactions with our dogs. This section concludes with a chapter about how to use problem solving to fix any agility issue that might arise.

If you are training your first agility dog, you might find that you are doing a number of things in these chapters that it would be best to change. I often joke with newer students that first agility dogs should be sainted, given all they put up with from us while we are learning. Thank goodness they are so forgiving!

21

Motivational Issues

When I used to publish an agility magazine, I received e-mails such as this one on occasion: "My dog started out loving agility. She was really fast. But now she doesn't want to do it at all. I have to beg her to do an obstacle. Where did I go wrong?"

None of us mean to turn our dogs off to agility. But sometimes we inadvertently do exactly that. There are ten behaviors that handlers sometimes engage in that are guaranteed to discourage a dog. We will consider those behaviors in this chapter and how to prevent them.

Learning to Dance

Before we think about our dogs, let's imagine that you are taking up an activity that is brand new—say square dancing. You know absolutely nothing about square dancing, but someone has told you it's fun, so you sign up for a beginner's class.

During your first few classes, you are really excited and have fun. But then the square dancing moves begin to get a little more complex. Sometimes you make a mistake. Your partner harrumphs, makes a bad face, and shakes her head. She wants to get it right, so she demands that you do the dance move over and over. She forgets to ever say anything nice to you or offer any positive reinforcement for your effort and improvement. In addition, the dances keep getting more and more difficult each week, although neither you nor your partner feels confident about the basics. Rather than taking pride in your growing skills, you feel lost and worried that you will make a mistake. When the beginner's class is over, you determine that square dancing is not for you and decide to try something less stressful.

The odds are good that every one of you has had a similar experience with your dogs. This is good to remember because agility handlers sometimes act like the unhappy square dance partner without thinking of the impact on the dog. Dogs are generally quite sensitive, and they respond exactly like we would by deciding on some level that they don't love the agility game. Just like

Dogs will grow to love an activity in which they feel encouraged and successful.

us, dogs will grow to love an activity in which they feel encouraged and successful. They will lose interest if they get discouraged, anxious, or feel there is not enough of a payoff.

Discouragement and anxiety show up in a variety of ways with dogs. They include refusing to run, slowing down, running away, running in circles, or stopping to sniff. If your dog is exhibiting any of these behaviors, take a break. Read this chapter with an open mind, and decide what you might be doing to de-motivate him. Switch gears right away, and become a partner with whom you would like to dance.

Ten De-Motivating Behaviors

When you read this list of ten things you can do to make agility less than fun for your dog, it may discourage *you* a bit. If you read one or more items from this list and recognize yourself, don't beat yourself up. Everyone, even the best in the world, has headed down the wrong path a few times. Just make a plan to change your behavior. Most dogs are resilient and will bounce back if you emphasize having fun together.

1.) Reacting Negatively

Dogs are body language experts. Your dog reads your movements and your facial expression every waking hour. He knows every tone of your voice. He knows when you are happy, and he knows

Solving Common Intermediate-Level Problems

when you are annoyed. He does *not* know how to distinguish when you are mad at yourself or mad at him.

When we are learning agility, we frequently make handler "mistakes." It is just the nature of the game. We send our dog over the wrong obstacle, or we pull him around a corner too quickly and he misses a jump. There are hundreds of possibilities. Keep in mind that these are mistakes only in your mind, not your dog's, because he doesn't know what the correct course is anyway. Interestingly, this is a difficult concept for many folks.

The question is, what do you do when something doesn't go as you had planned? For example, you meant to send your dog into a tunnel, but you sent him over a jump instead. Lots of folks stop in their tracks, frown, harrumph, groan, stamp, or say "Drat!" When you react in this way, the dog thinks that he has done something wrong, when in reality, all he did was try to figure out what you wanted.

> **Take Note**
> It is easy to slip into thinking that your dog is doing something wrong on purpose. However, dogs do a given behavior because it has the greatest chance of earning a cookie, or it is perceived as being safer. If your dog keeps taking a contact instead of a tunnel, for example, reinforce the tunnel more often by playing with him or tossing a hunk of cookie.

Every time you show physical and verbal displeasure in agility, it chinks at your dog's confidence. The doubt you create rears its head the next time the same situation or obstacle comes up: *Dogwalk? Did you say dogwalk? Am I hearing you right?* Repeat your behavior a few times with different obstacles, and the whole game becomes anxiety producing.

Solution

Stay happy. Laugh at mistakes. This is really hard, but remember, an off course is a human value. Your dog is just doing what he thinks you want. If he goes off course, say cheerily "Let's try that again!" If it has gone wrong several times, ask him to do something simple, like sit, and give him a cookie. Then figure out how to get the performance you originally wanted and reward, reward, reward.

2.) Abandoning Your Dog

Dogs are pack animals, and isolation is a negative experience for them. Yet here is a common scenario in agility classes: A student is running a series of obstacles. Something goes "wrong" in the middle of the course. The student stops running and walks over to the teacher to discuss the glitch. In doing this, she simply turns her back on her dog and walks away from him. He is left to wander off or sniff.

Think back to your square dancing experience, and imagine that you have just made a mistake. Without saying anything to you, your partner stops dancing, turns his back, and walks over to talk to the teacher. You are left standing alone with no idea what has gone wrong. This is how your dog feels.

Participating in trials is intense for dogs.

Solution

If you want to stop while running a sequence or course, call your dog kindly and ask him to do something easy, such as sit. Give him a cookie for that and quietly leash him up. The reinforcement and leashing—if done with no negative body language or annoyed noises—keeps your relationship intact. Then go talk with your teacher.

If you are a teacher, consider implementing a rule that students can't come discuss a sequence before they have reinforced their dog for playing the game and snapped on the leash.

3.) Asking for too Much too Fast in Class

Given the addictive nature of agility, it is very easy to push a dog too fast in several ways. The first is to ask him to do sequences that are too long for his level of confidence. This is often the result of plugging a dog into a class that is farther along in skill development and expecting him to keep up. Because he is not sure what he is doing, he will become anxious and start to shut down.

Solution

If you are in a class doing exercises that are a bit beyond your dog's skill level, just do the part of the exercise appropriate for your dog. This takes tremendous self-control on your part. Then find an opportunity at another time to isolate and teach your dog the more challenging skills using the methods we've discussed throughout the book.

Solving Common Intermediate-Level Problems

4.) Asking for too Much too Fast in Trials

Participating in trials is intense for dogs. Hundreds of dogs and many hours in a pen near strangers take its toll. I often observe that dogs who had fun initially are performing less happily in the second run or on the second day.

Solution

Enter just one class initially. Choose the easiest game for your dog, such as jumpers. Consider entering just one day for your first few events. Gradually increase the number of classes and days when your dog is happy and confident with what he has been doing.

5.) Forgetting Play

Early in agility training, most handlers are encouraged to use toys to reward their dogs. Dogs tug between exercises and pounce on their food bags after running through a tunnel. As they become more advanced, the toys disappear. In fact, it is common that the more we ask of a dog, the less we reinforce him in general.

Solution

Bring out your dog's toys in every class and at every trial. Play before he runs. Surprise him with a toss of a favorite flying disc or Nylabone toy in the middle of a long sequence several times in every class. Be a surprising and fun partner.

6.) Being Predictable with Rewards at Class

In an earlier chapter, we discussed the danger of rewarding only at the end of every sequence in practice, but it bears repeating. Why in the world should a dog hurry if he gets his toy or a cookie only after the last obstacle of a sequence?

Solution

Be surprising. Reinforce outstanding performances at any time. Reward running fast. Reward trying hard. Reward running ahead. Reward him for playing enthusiastically with you. While this seems quite obvious, I notice that students slide into the "reward at the end" pattern unless I remind them frequently. Any time your dog gets a behavior that has been a struggle or does something better than the time before, stop and pay him.

7.) Accepting Slow Performances

After all the talk of rewards, this one may seem like a contradiction. It isn't. The one thing you should not reinforce is a behavior that is slower than what you would like and than what your dog is capable of delivering. It is very possible to teach a dog that you actually want him to go slowly. I have watched a number of folks do this by rewarding every run even as the dog went slower and slower. The dogs learned that they could expend less energy and still get the cookies by staying right next to their handler.

Make every interaction with your dog enhance his joy at playing the game.

Solution

If your dog is lively at the beginning of a training session, stop before he slows down. It takes serious self-discipline to shorten your training sessions so that you stop before your dog tires. Some dogs tire mentally long before they tire physically. If your dog is slow consistently, experiment with strategies to excite him. If he loves food, get a bag from a dog-training supply company that's designed to be stuffed with delectable cookies. Fill it with special goodies. Use it to wind him up before he runs, and then surprise him by tossing it any time he speeds up. After you throw the bag, always run out, open it, and let him take a bite right out of it. If he likes a toy, use it before, during, and after runs.

8.) Delaying Rewards at Trials

I am constantly amazed that folks walk out of the ring at trials and march off with their dog, who gets nothing other than a "Good dog." By the time the handler gets back to her canopy, the run is a distant memory for the dog.

Solution

Each venue has a legal distance from the ring where you can place toys and cookies. Know that distance, and place your chair and cookies or toy near that spot. When you have leashed your dog

Solving Common Intermediate-Level Problems

and left the ring, race to your chair and throw a party for him. Don't chat with anyone else until you have told your partner how much you appreciate his effort.

9.) Conveying Anxiety
Not all of us have fun personalities. Sadly, I note that folks who smile little or seem nervous in general have dogs who do not perform well. Grim or anxious handlers have grim or anxious dogs. The fun factor is low, and the dogs pick up on this very quickly.

Solution
Think of agility as a personal growth experience. Smile at your dog. Be playful in ways that don't come naturally. Get down and roll around in the grass. Teach your dog interactive games like weaving through your legs that keep you busy and make you both happy.

10.) Practicing Excessively
During agility practices, there are times when you are working on a new handling move. For example, you might be working on the serpentine exercises. You get engrossed in getting it right yourself, and you may want to ask your dog to do the exercise over and over.

Solution
Generally, three or four times of any exercise is enough. If you seriously want to do more, take a break and do a different sequence or play a ball game. When you are both relaxed, come back for a few more repetitions. Then call it a day. End every training session with your dog happy and wanting more.

Concluding Thoughts
If your dog is motivated to play agility with you, this is a huge gift. Keep in mind when you train and trial that every interaction with your dog will either enhance his joy at playing the game with you or chip it away. If you can practice the positive handler behaviors described in this chapter, you will keep him loving the game. In fact, you will be the best dance partner your dog could ever ask for.

Exercise Adjustments
An effective agility teacher is able to adjust exercises to meet the needs of different students in the class. Never be shy about asking if you can simplify or shorten a sequence to maintain your dog's motivation.

Motivational Issues

22

Recapturing Lost Contacts

The odds are good that you have spent a great deal of time teaching your dog a contact behavior such as the two on/two off during his early training. Unfortunately, I have some bad news for you. No matter how good your dog's contact performance is in training, this behavior is likely to deteriorate once you start competing, something that many of you may already have discovered.

In this chapter, we will take a look at why this can happen, as well as discuss some intermediate training techniques to address this problem. We will also consider your options for retraining the behavior if necessary. Whatever you decide to do, it is important to remember that your dog's contact behavior is delicate at best, and it will require that you actively maintain it through his whole performance career.

As I have mentioned earlier, agility continues to evolve in many ways, but it is safe to say that the most dynamic changes have been in the area of contact performance. Agility competitors continue to strive to develop a fast and fail-safe strategy for getting their dogs to touch those feet in the contact zone. This has resulted in new methods to improve the two on/two off as well as the development of newer methods that show good promise.

Initially in this chapter, we will focus on issues with the two on/two off method because it has been the most popular method in recent years. If you have taught a different method, you may want to skip to the section of this chapter on new options.

Why Contact Behavior Deteriorates

The deterioration of the two on/two off contact performance takes two forms. Interestingly, they are polar opposites. Some dogs quit stopping altogether, and in their hurry to get to the

Contacts require ongoing maintenance.

next obstacle, they leap over the contact zone. This is exactly the behavior we hoped to prevent by teaching the two on/two off originally. A second issue is that dogs often start creeping down the contact obstacles, particularly the A-frame, in anticipation of having to stop. This eats up the seconds.

One thing we must admit: When things fall apart, it is always our own doing. What happens is that we teach the contacts in a certain way at school and then we become loose about enforcing or reinforcing our own rules in trial situations. We get excited and charge on to the next obstacle, whether our dog has done what we have asked or not. Here is the really bad news: A single instance of allowing your criteria to slip is usually enough to set the stage for contact troubles as early as the very next contact obstacle.

If you enforce the rules about contacts in training but not at trials, you will get great contacts in training and unreliable contacts at trials. As my teacher often says, dogs are very capable of having two completely separate sets of rules by which they behave, one reserved for class and another one when we are out in public.

How to Fix Contact Problems

There are two things that you can do to help keep your dog from developing two sets of rules or to help him understand that you want the same behavior all the time. First, if you want the same behavior from your dog in class and at trials, you need to start by acting the same with him in both places. Second, you need to devote time at trials to reinforce your dog for the behavior you want. Let's look at each of these in more depth.

Solving Common Intermediate-Level Problems

Synchronize Your Training and Trialing Behaviors

It is very common for people to work contacts in training in a way that is diametrically opposed to the way that they work them in trials. Consider the following:

- In training, do you ask your dog to hold his contacts for a long time (several seconds) 100 percent of the time?
- In training, do you give food and toy rewards 100 percent of the time?

If your answers are yes, consider how unlikely is it that you will do either of these regularly in a trial situation. When you do one thing in training and something completely different when competing, the dog quickly recognizes that the game has changed, and he decides that the old rules no longer apply.

Hitting the Up Contact
In some agility venues, the dog must run through the contact zone of the upside of the contact obstacle. For dogs with large strides, this can present a challenge. If your dog misses the up contact, try slowing down or even stopping very briefly as he approaches the obstacle. This often causes dogs to hesitate just long enough to put a foot in the right place.

Practice Quick Releases

Let's look at how you can align your training and trialing. In trials, most handlers do quick releases. This means that the handler asks for the two on/two off but then releases the dog to the next obstacle the second he hesitates in the correct position. The handler's verbal command sounds like "touchokay." The quick release is a good trial behavior because it propels the dog forward quickly. Most dogs who have a well-trained two on/two off do this naturally once or twice. Then they realize that there has been no reinforcement in the form of a cookie or even a kind word for stopping. Before long, they decide that there is no need to hesitate at all. This quickly translates to striding or jumping off the contact obstacle above the contact zone.

The answer is relatively simple. If you are going to do quick releases at trials rather than asking your dog to hold his contact for a second or two, you need to practice quick releases on a regular basis in training also. Ideally, your training should be a good balance of quick releases and longer holds in which your dog maintains the two on/two off for several seconds. A good balance in practice is 50 percent quick release contacts and 50 percent longer holds.

Reconsider Your Reward System

To further align training and trials, you need to reconsider your reward system. As I mentioned earlier, handlers often fall into a pattern of rewarding every good contact in class with a cookie. As a result, many dogs have great contacts in class. Then when the dog goes to a trial, he gets no reinforcement when he holds his contact. On the flip side, he rewards himself when he races on because he gets to do that next obstacle. He has effectively learned that the only thing that earns a reward is racing ahead, which may include leaping over the contact zone.

Recapturing Lost Contacts

Take the time to say "What a good boy you are!"

This situation is fixable. Because you can't use cookies in shows, you need to modify your reinforcement system to include something that you can use in both places. The only things you have available are verbal praise and your expression. When in class or at a show, you need to take the time to say "What a good boy you are." Add a smile. This is the ultimate in human self-control because competing makes us want to bolt forward.

Putting It All Together

Let's look at a system on page 191 that you can use that will increase your odds of having reliable contacts in class and at trials. With the plan I am sharing, I am assuming that your dog is already solid with holding his contact in class. Then you are ready to transition to a plan such as this.

It is useful to ask a friend to observe or videotape you doing this practice to ensure that when you want your dog to hold the contact, he is not releasing before you tell him. You can also check that you are praising him. This is the time to be very honest with yourself and make sure that you are being consistent with your criteria. This teaches him that the rules apply whether you are doing fast releases or long holds.

Reinforce Contacts at Trials

It is easy to say while sitting here, but of course we are not the same when we get hyped up on course. The reality is that every time we go on course, we make dozens of choices. The important thing is that you are aware of what you are doing and that there are consequences. If you let your dog forget the rules on one contact, it is not fair to expect him to get it right on the following contacts.

Solving Common Intermediate-Level Problems

In Class		
Hold the contact (50% of time)	Reward with cookies half of the repetitions by dropping them on the ground as your dog holds the two on/two off. Verbally praise half of the repetitions.	
Quick releases (50% of time)	Half of the time, ask for the two on/two off behavior. As soon as your dog hits the correct position, mark it with your clicker and release him immediately by tossing a cookie or toy forward. Half of the time, ask for the two on/two off behavior. As soon as he hits it, release him and go on to the next obstacle.	
In Trials		
Hold the contact (50% of time)	Verbally praise the behavior: "You are the best dog in the whole world!" Smile. Then release to the next obstacle.	
Quick releases (50% of time)	Release your dog the second he hits his contact. He is reinforced by getting to go on to the next obstacle.	

I can hear what you are thinking. *What if I do try to get my dog's contact performance correct in a trial or in training and he doesn't stop in the correct position, or he leaps over the contact zone, or he bolts for the next obstacle before I release him?* For starters, it will happen. It happens to everyone sooner or later.

As soon as the behavior breaks down, you have three options. The first one is appropriate for training classes or venues that allow you to redo contacts. It works particularly well for high-drive dogs who want to keep playing because it slows down the game, which they don't like. The second two can be used at trials that do not allow redos.

- If your dog misses the contact, get his attention and put him in the *heel* position. Walk him around to the start of the contact. Be slow and deliberate. Ask him to do the contact obstacle again. If he gets it right, reinforce generously. If he makes a second mistake, it's likely that he doesn't know or has forgotten how to do what you are asking. You will need to take some time to retrain the behavior and reward generously when he gets this behavior right.
- If your dog charges off or jumps over the contact, stand perfectly still. Let him come back to you. Don't say anything. Stand still some more. If he barks at you, ignore it or you will be letting him boss you around. Stand as long as you can stand it. When you are ready, continue your run. Ask your dog to stop on the next contact. Praise liberally if he does.
- Stop your run and excuse yourself. Walk off course quietly and put your dog away. I am often skeptical that dogs understand this strategy. I think that the dog has no idea why he is being walked off the course. However, you might try it once and see if the behavior improves. If not, assume that your dog really does not understand what he is supposed to do, and retrain away before you trial again.

Of course, these strategies work only if you have the discipline to do them as many times as your dog requires. If you are random and sporadic, your dog will just be confused.

Recapturing Lost Contacts

One contact problem you may encounter is that your dog may anticipate the stop at the bottom of the contact and creep down.

Play the "De-Stick" Game

Just when you have taught your dog the two on/two off position, he may surprise you with a new issue: He may start anticipating the stop at the bottom of the contact. This translates into a slow, creeping descent or even an early stop above the contact zone. We inadvertently reinforce this creep by focusing on the two on/two off behavior and rewarding our dogs when they stop in the correct position, regardless of the speed with which they get there.

When your dog shows this behavior, you can play "de-stick" lessons. These exercises are appropriate only in cases where the dog has considerable experience performing the two on/two off correctly in the past and then has suddenly begun creeping to the bottom in his performance. The best idea is to play this game with him before he starts to stick.

In this game, you are going to start by letting your dog run through the contact without stopping. This may seem risky, and it is because it is exactly the opposite of what you have taught, but other strategies don't work very well. I have tried surprise food targets at the bottom of the contacts to hurry dogs, but they quickly became wise and raced to the bottom only if they saw the cookies. I have experimented positioning a friend off to the side of the contact and having her toss a cookie at the bottom if the dog hurried. Every dog quickly became wise to this system too.

Step 1

This part of the game is to simply free your dog up and get him moving again.
1. Start with a big hunk of cookie or your dog's favorite toy in your hand, like a Nylabone, as you send him over the A-frame or dogwalk.

Solving Common Intermediate-Level Problems

2. As he approaches the bottom of the contact, sweep it through the contact zone and toss it forward without making him stop.
3. Use a command, such as the *get it* command rather than your normal release word, as he approaches the bottom. You will need that again later.
4. Repeat this over several sessions.

He may stop the first few times from habit, but then he will get the idea that he gets reinforced only for running forward. With several repetitions, you should see him speed up as he runs to the bottom and off.

When I started this game with my young dog, she got so excited when I brought out the toy that she started leaping the contact zone. I added a PVC hoop to keep her head down so that she had to stay on the whole way to the bottom of the contact obstacle. You may need to do the same. You want your dog to run through the contact zone, not jump over it.

Step 2

Now you are going to bring back your two on/two off but continue to give your dog a reason to hustle to the bottom. You will start this as soon as he is running down and off the obstacle at full speed.

1. To tell your dog that you want him to stop, put a small food target at the bottom of the A-frame or dogwalk. You may need to show it to him the first time or two because he is now used to racing forward and may not see it.
2. Continue to carry another hunk of cookie or his toy as you have been doing.
3. Send your dog over the obstacle and give him the *two on/two off* command.
4. The second he has wolfed the cookie on the ground, toss the second cookie or toy forward so that he drives forward. Use his regular release word now.

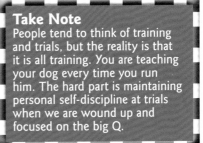

Take Note
People tend to think of training and trials, but the reality is that it is all training. You are teaching your dog every time you run him. The hard part is maintaining personal self-discipline at trials when we are wound up and focused on the big Q.

This is a fun game for dogs because they get paid twice in quick succession. If at any point in this practice your pup returns to creeping, return to the first step and let him run off a few times. Then return to asking for the two on/two off. Keep the game high energy and fun.

Step 3

At the next level, eliminate the cookie lure at the bottom of the contact. When your dog stops in the two on/two off, alternate tossing a cookie to him in that position to remind him that he should still stop or immediately release him forward with a toy or cookie toss. By mixing it up, you give him a reason to get to hustle down because he doesn't know if he will be stopping for a bit or running forward. If you see any creeping return, place greater emphasis on releasing him forward for his reinforcement.

New Contact Options

For years, it seemed as if the two on/two off was *it*, the answer to perfect, reliable contacts. As I mentioned earlier, there are now more options to consider, each with its pros and cons.

If your dog has struggled for a time with his performance or has developed two sets of rules that you find difficult to change, you may want to retrain using a different method. For example, I spent a year teaching my young Sheltie a solid two on/two off. After too many quick releases at a national event, he never regained his previous reliability with the two on/two off. I opted to retrain him using the modified running contact described in this section. This was successful, although I know that this new behavior is fragile as well.

There are two new approaches that appear to have the most promise. Either of these should be taught with the assistance of someone familiar with the process.

Running Contact

This strategy focuses on teaching the dog to run full speed to the bottom of the A-frame and dogwalk without stopping at all. This is a nice idea and looks fabulous when performed correctly, although a serious debate exists about whether all dogs can successfully master it. A great deal of experimentation in training running contacts is in progress, particularly among those who hope to compete successfully at the national level.

In Linda Mecklenberg's definitive series of articles (*Clean Run Magazine*, February 2003) on running contacts, she was vehement that dogs must come with the correct natural stride length or " . . . they will never reliably stride into the contact using this technique." The technique to which she referred involved placing horizontal devices called stride regulators across the contact zone of the A-frame or dogwalk to help the dogs learn how to step in the correct spot. More recently, she writes, "That doesn't mean that you can't teach a running contact if the dog does not have a natural stride for it; I have two dogs now (Border Collies) who have running A-frames and running dogwalks, and they are quite consistent." Rachel Sanders, an international team member, became fascinated with great running contacts she saw in Europe. When she came home, she set about to develop a system to replicate that behavior. She developed a system in which dogs are taught to spring in and out of a "box" made with plastic pipe that is the same size as the A-frame contact zone. Gradually, this box is moved onto the downside of the obstacle and the dog continues to spring into the box, thereby hitting the center of the contact. (See www.fastforwarddogsports.com for a video example.)

It will take time to determine if the running contact is a viable choice for most competitors. On the other hand, there are times that the running contact is the correct choice. For all dogs with long backs, such as Corgis, slamming into a stop can be downright dangerous. Aging dogs and those with straight shoulders can get sore from frequent stops. After five years of stopping, my straight-shouldered Sheltie, Scout, developed a chronically sore front end. Once I transitioned to a running contact, she came back strong and fast. For an experienced dog like Scout or dogs who are not prone to leaping, teaching a running contact can be as simple as using a hoop at the end of the contact to keep the dog's head down and moving the target, a cookie or toy, several feet (m) from the end of the obstacle so that he has to run out to get it.

Solving Common Intermediate-Level Problems

One new contact option consists of teaching a dog to run full speed just past the bottom of the contact equipment and then lie down or crouch very briefly within a body length of the contact.

My caution is that if you select a running contact, it needs to be taught, not just be the result of giving up once your behavior of choice has been lost. Once dogs learn that they don't have to stop or at least hesitate, they may quickly learn that they can sail right over the contact zone.

Modified Running Contact (Four on the Floor)

Another interesting contact strategy was developed in recent years by competitor Ann Croft. This strategy consists of teaching the dog to run full speed just past the bottom of the contact equipment and then lie down or crouch very briefly within a body length of the contact. In contrast to the two on/two off, in which the dog continues to touch the contact with his back feet, the dog runs right off the contact obstacle before he stops.

This method offers a mix of benefits. Stopping the dog on the flat eliminates jamming the front end, which is inevitable on the A-frame with a quick dog. It also keeps him from starting to creep down the contact because he is quickly rewarded for running off the bottom and lying down. It is proving to be a viable choice with dogs who simply couldn't master the two on/two off for different reasons.

In her video, Ann Croft walks viewers through steps that include developing toy drive (dogs must want to run out to something motivational), teaching the dog to run under a hoop to run with his head down, and teaching him to run up and over the obstacle and under the hoop. Separately, she teaches the dog to lie down on a target. Last, she pairs these behaviors so that the dog runs down and off the obstacle and briefly lies down. On the downside, some trainers with very athletic dogs report that their partners can leap off the contact and still land in a *down*. This becomes much more difficult if you keep the target quite close to the contact.

It will take some time to see how this method holds up in trials. At this point in time, the strategy seems promising.

Concluding Thoughts

It seems likely that teaching fast, reliable contacts will remain the center stage issue through the rest of my agility career and yours. Select a method that fits your dog best, teach it well, and then maintain, maintain, maintain. If things start to deteriorate, stop what you are doing before your dog gets it wrong too many times. Breathe. Make a plan to retrain him, and follow through in classes and at trials.

23

Reteaching the Stay

Consider how often you have seen the following from your dog or another dog at an agility trial:

- Mark orders his Border Collie to "wait" at the start. By the time Mark reaches the first obstacle, Zip has broken his *stay*, blasted past him, and is making up his own course.
- Marsha leaves her Sheltie, who immediately begins scooting forward on his rear end. When she notices her dog's forward motion, she calls him before she is in the right position on the course.

The *stay* command is generally the first behavior to disappear or deteriorate when handlers start running longer sequences and begin trialing. This puts the intermediate handler at a serious disadvantage on courses that often start with a discrimination or challenging angles.

It is helpful to understand why things go wrong with this basic command. Then we'll consider how you can reteach the *stay* so that it is reliable in class and at trials.

Not all *Stays* Are Created Equal

The demands of the *stay* required for obedience and agility are very different. In obedience, *stay* requires inaction on the dog's part. The handler leaves quietly and returns quietly. In agility, the picture changes completely. The dog must stay while resisting a tremendous temptation to run and jump, even though he knows exactly what is coming. I compare this situation to asking a child to sit perfectly still while facing Disneyland—even the most compliant youngster who can sit still at home or in school would find this impossible. The bottom line is that the agility *stay* requires a completely different kind of self-control from a dog than the obedience *stay* does.

Despite this difference, many trainers who are preparing their dog for agility count on the traditional method of teaching the *stay* command. That is, the trainer sits the dog and puts him back where he was if he changes position. The dog "learns" to stay, but he is often not happy or comfortable with the command.

Then there is a predictable scenario that evolves once the dog comes to agility classes. At first, he sits quietly behind a jump when asked to stay. But over a few weeks and months, he starts to get excited about the game. He wants to run and jump. He starts to notice that he is always going to be released from his *stay* to run forward. The *stay* becomes an annoying delay. He waits until the handler gets to a certain point on course and then he makes the decision to get started. He breaks his *stay* and takes the first obstacle or sometimes races around it to get to the handler.

When this happens, the handler stops the dog and returns him to his position behind the first obstacle. If you return a dog enough times to the start line in practice, he is likely to get a reliable *stay* in class, but there is still the potential underlying problem that the dog is being only superficially compliant but lacks real self-control.

Then the new handler arrives at her first trial with this tenuous *stay*. We mix in a good batch of trial adrenalin for both dog and human, and the stage is set for disaster. The handler enters the ring, puts the dog in a *sit-stay* at the line, and leads out. Before she is ready, her dog, who knows exactly what is coming, blasts off the line and starts taking obstacles. Guess what the handler does? She runs to catch up. After all, this is a show. The dog is effectively reinforced for launching himself into the game. Once a dog has done this once or twice, any semblance of a *stay* is gone, gone, gone.

This can happen at any time. I know because my Sheltie Scout had a solid *stay* for the first two years of her agility career. Each trial she grew in confidence until one day, she walked into the ring and sat, but before I could take two steps away, she was off and running. Want to guess what I did? I ran. For the next several years, I had no *stay* in trials. Naturally, she stayed perfectly in class. I tried everything I could think of to recapture the command, from standing still when she ran and telling her I wasn't going to play to wheeling around and walking off the course as described in the previous chapter. Nothing worked consistently. Scout and I even competed in the finals of a national event, in which the video on the Internet showed me holding her chest hair lightly at the start line to keep her from taking off and then racing her to the first obstacle. It was far from a professional start.

There are two things to consider if you want a *stay* you can count on. First, there is another method for teaching an agility *stay* that has a much greater chance of holding up. Second, there is something you can do to reinforce *stay* in a trial setting.

Take Note

When my students' dogs break their *stays*, they often say "He knows how to stay." Yes he does, but only in certain circumstances. Knowing how to stay at home or at obedience class does not mean that he knows how to stay in agility. Agility requires a dog to stay when he is at his most stimulated. This takes a special kind of self-control that you can teach with time and patience.

Solving Common Intermediate-Level Problems

Teaching *Stay* in a New Way

There is a way to teach your dog to stay in an entirely different way that teaches him that *stay* is an integral part of the game, not something difficult he has to do before he gets to play. It creates confidence instead of anxiety. The method I am going to describe works for both low-drive and high-drive dogs. It works because it teaches the dog self-control even when he is excited. It also teaches him to remain alert during the *stay* because something fun is going to happen.

This game assumes three things:

1. You have already taught your dog to sit on cue using positive reinforcement with a toy or cookies.
2. You and your dog can play together with a toy or just running around.
3. If you use a tug toy, your dog knows how to give the toy to you on command.

A surprising number of dogs don't know how to play with their owner. This is a key to getting your dog revved up for this game. Take time to make sure that you can play interactively. Tug is a great game as long as you are in charge of starting and stopping the play.

Step 1

The basis of this game is to teach your dog that sitting and staying are as much fun and as rewarding as interacting with the obstacles. Even if you have already taught a *stay* command, you are now going to stop using that command and just use the *sit* to tell your dog that he is going to stay seated until asked to do something else.

23.A: Start a game with your dog.

23.B: While in the midst of play mode, quickly tell your dog to sit.

23.C: The moment he sits, toss your toy or cookie off to the side.

Reteaching the *Stay*

1. Start a game with your dog. (See Photo 23.A.) It needs to be something that gets him energized, such as playing with a tug toy or running and romping with you. Do whatever you need to do to get your dog excited and playing with you.
2. While in the midst of play mode, quickly tell your dog to sit. (See Photo 23.B.) This is asking for self-control in the midst of excitement, just like at a trial.
3. The moment your dog sits, release him and toss your toy or cookie off to the side or slightly behind him. (See Photo 23.C.) If you are using cookies, it should be something big and easily visible to him, such as chunks of string cheese. The location of the toss is also very important—you want your dog to understand that he may get rewarded when he runs to the side or backward and not just when he runs forward.

For this game, use a release word other than your usual word. This will keep your dog from getting confused about the direction he should travel. When my pup hears "get it," she knows that she will be running to the side or back. When she hears "okay," she knows that she should drive forward over the obstacle.

Play this game over several days. Your dog should be visibly excited and enjoying this interaction because the point is for him to see the *stay* as a game.

Step 2

In the second phase, you will start to build distance from your dog very slowly.
1. Start the game as you have been doing by getting your dog excited and then asking him to sit.
2. When his bottom hits the ground, take one step away before releasing him and tossing the reinforcement. Your step away should be followed by your toy toss very quickly.
3. If your dog gets up, quietly move toward him and ask him to sit. Resist the urge to say "No!" If you feel compelled to talk, say something like "Uh oh" in a cheery tone. Resist the urge to lean over him in a threatening manner. Your goal is to get the right behavior and reward it rather than disciplining your dog.
4. As soon as he returns to sitting, take a quick step away, release him, and toss the toy or cookie back to him.

Step 3

Very gradually expand on Step 2 by extending the number of steps you take away from your dog. (See Photo 23.D.)
1. Take two steps away for a few days, then three and then four.
2. Continue to toss the toy or cookie back either off to the side or behind your dog. (See Photo 23.E.) This will tell him that he will get rewarded even when you are a distance away.
3. If your dog stands up before you release him, tell him "Uh oh!" Take a moment to collect yourself. Then ask him to sit but with no verbal or physical correction. Back away but not quite as far. Release him to get his toy. If you follow this plan, he will learn that breaking early delays the game. However, your dog should make only the occasional error. If frequent errors occur, you have gone too far too fast in teaching the rules of the game.

As you are able to increase your distance from your dog, continue to vary how far you go. Even

Solving Common Intermediate-Level Problems

23.D: Gradually extend the number of steps you take away from your dog.
23.E: Continue to toss the toy or cookie back either off to the side or behind him.

if you can get 10 feet (3 m) away, sometimes release him after two steps. The more unpredictable you keep the game, the more he will respond with intensity and joy.

Step 4

Once your dog will let you get at least 10 feet (3 m) away, it is time to make the game more complex. (See Photo 23.F.) At this level, you will add agility equipment.

1. Start by having your dog sit behind an agility jump.
2. Play the game exactly as you have been doing. Make sure to toss his toy beside or behind him so that he doesn't take the jump. (See Photo 23.G.) This will reinforce the belief that staying is as much fun as blasting forward. For two or three sessions, don't encourage him to jump at all.

Step 5

1. When your dog is staying like a rock, alternate the game you have been playing with calling him over the jump. (See Photo 23.H.)
2. Reward him behind the jump at least half the time.

   In this phase, you may add in the element of sometimes behaving more like you will in a trial. Lead out purposefully and position your hands as you will when competing. Release your dog backward sometimes and forward over the obstacle sometimes.

Step 6

It's time for proofing. Find a fun match that allows toys or cookies on course, and act as if you are at a trial. Set your dog up on the line and then reward him behind the jump as you have been doing. On subsequent runs, alternate rewarding your partner behind the first obstacle and calling him forward over the first obstacle. Remember to remain unpredictable. Your dog will quickly learn to break his *stay* again if you always call him over the jump the second time you lead out. Don't revert to using your old *stay* command.

Reteaching the *Stay*

23.F: Once your dog will let you get 10 feet (3 m) away, it's time to make the game more complex.

23.G: Make sure to toss his toy behind him so that he doesn't take the jump.

23.H: Alternate the game you have been playing with calling your dog over the jump.

Reinforcing *Stay* at Trials

As we discussed in the chapter on contacts, you can train until the cows come home, but you need to have a specific plan about how to continue your training in trials. Otherwise, all your good work will be gone in a heartbeat.

If you train your dog initially using the method just described and reinforce him regularly by playing the same game whenever you can, he may never break a *stay* at a trial because he thinks that the *sit* (with an implied *stay*) is exciting. On the other hand, he is likely to recognize that there is no cookie or toy toss at trials and give breaking the *sit* a try at least once. If your dog has already learned to break his *sit* at trials and you have retrained using this method, you can be sure that he will try to take off again. After all, it worked before. You need to expect this and make a plan so that it is not successful.

Enter the Right Venue

Enter a trial in one of the venues that allows you to return and reposition your dog at the start line. Both the North American Dog Agility Council, Inc. (NADAC), and Dogs on Course in North America (DOCNA) allow you to return to your dog and put him back in a *sit* if he breaks. The American Kennel Club (AKC) allows you to return and reposition your dog, but you may not lead out again. Because there are variations in how this is handled by different organizations, ask the judge to explain exactly what you may do if your dog breaks during your briefing.

Remain Calm

When you enter the ring for your runs, remind yourself that you cannot run if your dog breaks. If you succumb to the excitement, all your hard work will be gone. Put your dog in his *sit*. Lead out. If he holds, tell him he is a good dog. Then release him and go. If he breaks, immediately

Solving Common Intermediate-Level Problems

walk back to the start line. Be neutral physically and don't talk. Gently tell him to sit right where he was. Lead out again. If he holds, tell him he is a good dog. Release and go. Repeat this procedure every time you run.

After retraining Scout, I followed this plan. Because Scout had been abandoning her *stay* for a long time, she took off at least ten times over several trials and tackled the first jump. I returned her to the line each time. On the 11th run, she held tight. I told her what a good girl she was, and off we went. Her *stay* held for months. It was wonderful to be able to lead out and run a course without a mad dash of a start. Then one day, she forgot herself and took off. Fortunately, I was ready. Because this was not a venue that allowed me to return her to the start line, I just walked quietly off course. She followed me sadly. I am not a big fan of whisking dogs off course because they generally don't know what they have done wrong, but in this case, I knew that she knew. I quietly put her in her pen and left her. Since then, she has held like a rock at trial after trial. I know that someday she may forget herself, so each time I run, I practice what I will do before I get on course. But right now, I cannot imagine a better investment than finding that *stay*.

Develop a Reinforcement System

Recently, I had another ah ha! moment when watching an excellent DVD about exercises with one jump from Susan Garrett, a top Canadian teacher and competitor. Susan observed handlers delivering reinforcement cookies to their dogs after they had led out beyond one jump. What she saw was that the handlers reinforced their dogs when they were just beyond the jump, but once they had moved out farther, the cookies were few and far between. This may be because handlers feel that they need to hurry in a class situation or because they can't throw that far. Whatever the reason, this teaches dogs that they may as well take off once you get to a certain distance because there is little chance of a cookie coming their way. Susan suggests that you develop a system of reinforcing your dog so that he has an equal chance of a reward no matter how far you have gone. This strategy will definitely encourage him to stay.

Concluding Thoughts

Once you have taught your dog to stay using this new system, I would recommend that you play phases one through five regularly as part of your training routine. It is worth the investment. You may find that you have replaced a dog who is confused or anxious, or who never really understood the *stay*, with a dog who truly enjoys the *stay* and is alert for the next part of the game.

24
Effective Problem-Solving Techniques

In a recent class, a young Golden Retriever refused to go up the ramp to the dogwalk although he had been racing across that obstacle for several weeks. His body language said that he was clearly anxious about running up that narrow board.

When setbacks in training occur, handlers are frequently disappointed. This is simply human. On some level, we imagine our training progressing day by day until we have the perfect canine partner. In your dreams. In reality, you are much more likely to arrive at a day when your dog becomes apprehensive about some piece of equipment that he nailed just days before, decides that the tenth pole is a fine place to pop out, starts knocking bars, begins leaping over the contact zones, or decides that the top of the A-frame is the perfect place for striking a pose. The list of training challenges you may encounter is lengthy. There are simply no cookie-cutter methods of training that will take your dog from point A to point Z with no setbacks.

The problem is that when our dogs suddenly can't perform an obstacle that they have done well before or run a sequence we thought they had mastered, our first response is often to think that they are simply being stubborn or choosing to ignore us. This is a dangerous thought. Once a handler latches onto this idea, the next step is to try to fix the problem by getting stern and ordering the dog to get it right. This always makes the situation worse because the dog gets worried, and a worried dog is not in a state of mind to learn or relearn anything.

Why Setbacks Occur

Before we talk about how you can deal with setbacks from a positive frame of mind, let's consider why they occur. In general, there are five reasons:

1. Your dog may be hurt. For example, dogs often become reluctant to jump if their neck, toe, or back hurts. Always rule out physical reasons before you continue training.

The list of training challenges you may encounter is lengthy, but creative problem solving can help.

2. A dog may have gotten scared on an obstacle.
3. Your dog may not be getting enough payoff in terms of playtime or treats for completing a certain behavior. This is often true of jumps and tunnels, which we tend to take for granted, while we lavish praise and rewards at the contacts.
4. Your dog may not have learned the behavior as thoroughly as you thought. It takes hundreds of repetitions in multiple locations before dogs really know a behavior. They are not great at generalizing.
5. You may be doing something with your body language that is confusing your dog. As you may remember from *The Beginner's Guide to Dog Agility*, for example, we often teach our dogs to pull out at the tenth pole by changing the length of our stride or bolting forward.

There are also occasions when you will simply never know for sure what is worrying your dog. A friend's mixed breed began skittering around the teeter even though he had not had a bad experience of which the handler was aware. Whether you know the origin of the problem or not, your response should be the same: problem solve, problem solve, problem solve.

Teaching the Problem-Solving Model

Most of us are familiar with problem solving away from agility. First, we pose questions about a problem. Next, we brainstorm some possible solutions. We then select the solutions that make

Solving Common Intermediate-Level Problems

the most sense. Finally, we try one or more of the strategies and see if they work. If not, we adjust and try something else.

In agility, I have found that there are some questions that are particularly useful when things have not gone as you planned: Is there something the handler might be doing that is causing the problem? Has the dog had a recent bad experience? What can the handler do to make the task easier for the dog? What can the handler do to make the task inviting? What can the handler do to set up the dog for success? Is there a way to give the task a new look so that the dog thinks it is a different task?

Let's take a look at a few situations in which my students and I applied the problem-solving model.

Scenario #1: Missing Jumps

A friend's Labrador Retriever began running around the first jump when the handler began to lead out beyond the jump. Clearly, the dog saw the jump as a barrier to getting to the handler as quickly as possible. When we asked what the handler might be doing to cause the problem, the answer was simple: He never rewarded the first jump. As a result, the dog saw little point in bothering with it. So we asked ourselves how we could make the task inviting.

How to Solve It

We made two changes. First, we put the jump bar on the ground so that the dog didn't see it as a barrier. Then the handler started using his clicker every time the dog passed through the jump stanchions rather than running around. The click was, of course, followed with reinforcement, which in his case was a toss of the dog's toy. In short order, the Lab saw that his handler cared about him taking the jump and that he could still get to the handler just as quickly if he took the "jump." Once this mindset had been created, we gradually raised the bar. The dog has remained very reliable about taking the first jump. However, the handler has stopped taking the behavior for granted. Every now and then, he remembers to mark and reinforce this behavior for his dog.

Scenario #2: Fear of the Dogwalk

So what about that Golden Retriever from earlier in the chapter who had become fearful of the dogwalk? When I started asking questions, it turned out that the handler had taken him to a new facility to train. The dogwalk ramp was very springy, creating more motion than he was used to. After running over it once, the Golden became unwilling to get on the obstacle again. Now he was anxious even about the familiar dogwalk. Clearly, he wanted to comply with his handler's request, but he was afraid because of his bad experience.

How to Solve It

We tried a simple intervention: putting cookies across the dogwalk so that the pup could "graze" all the way across, as he did when he was first learning the obstacle. But even this did not encourage him to get onto it. At this point, we asked ourselves how we could change the look of the task so that he would see our request as something new.

We decided to put the 24-inch (61-cm) table under the end of the incline ramp. This caused the ramp to look almost flat and hopefully unlike the "goblin dogwalk." We asked the dog to jump up onto the table where we knew he felt confident. I then held him on the table facing the dogwalk. The handler walked to the other end and walked up the dogwalk ramp just a bit toward the dog. Her voice encouraged him to come forward. When he was focused on her, I released him and off he went. The handler backed off the dogwalk as her dog approached. (This obviously takes some good balance, so bring in a steady friend if necessary.) The Golden made it across with only a hint of anxiety. We repeated the same format over several classes until all signs of fearfulness were gone. Then we started again, with the ramp on a 20-inch (51-cm) table and then on a 16-inch (40.5-cm) table. At that point, it was clear that he was ready to return to performing the obstacle without props.

Scenario #3

One of the most challenging and persistent problems is knocking bars. Some dogs are prone to knocking bars all the time. Others send the bars flying only in trials when they are excited. It is particularly sad to have an otherwise perfect run turn into a disqualification when a bar comes down.

How to Solve It

Start by making sure that your dog is physically comfortable with the height he is being asked to jump. If he is, the next step is to ask whether the handler is doing something to cause the dog to hit the bar. The most common handler errors that cause a dog to hit bars are crowding him, blocking his path, making a jerky motion, giving a late cue, or talking to him while he is in the air. This question of whether the handler is causing the problem can be answered by videotaping a run and analyzing it. If you can identify what you are doing to cause the problem, rejoice. Those are easy to fix. Stay farther away so that you are out of his path. Stay quiet. Cue early. This will make you a better handler in general too.

There are times that the handler can be doing everything right, but the bars are flying. In general, this is because the dog's jumping style is so flat that he clips the bar, or he gets so excited to move forward that he does not see clearing the bar as important. The question now becomes how you can set up the dog for success.

Solving Common Intermediate-Level Problems

To counter fear of the dogwalk, the author put a 24-inch (61-cm) table under the end of the incline ramp.

Play a simple jumping game with your dog regularly. This teaches him that you like it when he clears the bar. Have his favorite toy in hand, like a Nylabone, and a single jump. Send him over the jump from fairly close. If he clears it, play like mad. If he ticks it or knocks it, say "Uh oh" and withhold the toy. Send him over again and reinforce immediately if successful. When he consistently clears one jump, gradually start from farther back to increase speed. When he is successful with one jump from 15 feet (4.5 m), add a second jump. Over time, add additional jumps and distance. Any time he knocks a bar, the game stops. Any time he clears all of the bars, throw a party.

If the bar-knocking problem persists, you may need additional help. Seek the advice of an experienced teacher. In addition, there are a growing number of specialized videos to help handlers work through specific problems. For example, jumping expert Susan Salo offers many exercises on her DVDs to help dogs learn the mechanics of successful jumping. This is a great way to supplement your class instruction.

Mental Practice

Your imagination is the only limit as you consider how to help your dog understand the agility game. For example, in Scenario #2 earlier, some of you may have thought of using x-pens on either side of that first jump to show the Lab the path the handler wanted. Good idea. What might you do for the following challenges?

Effective Problem-Solving Techniques

- Your dog starts refusing to sit or down on the table.
- Your dog is anxious about judges and really anxious about judges wearing hats.
- Your dog always chooses the contact obstacle when you are working a discrimination.

If your dog refuses the *sit* or *down*:

- Work on *sit* away from the table. Use your clicker and high-value treats. Make this a fun, high-energy game. When you put the game back onto the table, maintain the same fun approach. After you click and reinforce, release immediately without a *stay*. Gradually reintroduce the five-second *stay*, but don't do it every time your dog gets onto the table.

- Change your dog's picture about the table as a boring place. Teach him a trick he can do on the table. Teach it to him away from the table. Then ask him to do the trick on the table and celebrate. This can be a simple trick like a spin. After he has done this several times, ask for the *sit*. Immediately click, reinforce, and release. This will often cause a dog to forget that he didn't want to sit. Gradually fade the trick, but make sure that he gets lots of reinforcement when he sits quickly.
- If you have two dogs who like each other, create a table competition. Send them both to the table, give your command, and reinforce the dog who sits most quickly. If one dog always wins, reinforce both for a lively response. This is a favorite winter game in our house.

The next issue is a bit easier. If your dog is afraid of judges in hats, visit the local secondhand clothing store. Buy hats in every size and shape. At every class, ask a different classmate to wear a different hat and stand on the course while you run.

The third issue has at least three solutions to consider:

- Evaluate your cueing system as we have discussed in previous chapters. Are you using a consistent system to clearly tell your dog which obstacle you want? If the answer is no, you may fix this problem by fixing your handling.
- If your communication is clear but your dog continues to make this mistake, a second option is to bring out your gate to block the contact obstacle. Then, when he "chooses" the other obstacle, reinforce him as generously as you do for the contact. Repeat over several sessions.
- A third option is to have a friend stand near the contact and swing a jump bar across the contact like a slow windshield wiper until your dog passes. Again reinforce for the correct performance. Repeat several times.

Whatever happens with your dog, remember to deal with it positively. If you communicate frustration to your partner, you will always make the situation worse.

Solving Common Intermediate-Level Problems

Your imagination is the only limit to helping your dog.

Concluding Thoughts

From your first day of training your dog, expect things to go awry. This will keep you from getting frustrated with your dog, which chips away at your relationship. As long as he stays healthy, most things are fixable.

Sometimes handlers want to keep pressing on with methods that are clearly not working. If your current method stops working, stop right away. Relax. Ask questions and problem solve, problem solve, problem solve.

The odds are good that if you are interested in intermediate agility skills, you are already competing with your dog in one or more venues or are planning to take the leap soon. Although there is no hurry, most folks who stick with the sport decide to go out and test themselves and their dog in an official trial.

One of the unique things about agility is the proliferation of different agility organizations, each with a different style and atmosphere. Canine Performance Events (CPE) has held onto its philosophy that teams should have fun while earning titles. The United States Dog Agility Association (USDAA) prides itself in promoting the highest-level international standards for the sport. Each of the other agility organizations offers programs with their own slant on the sport.

In more densely populated areas, there are so many trials that it has become necessary to pick and choose what to enter. I find that most of my students and friends pick a favorite venue on which to focus and then compete in other organizations when it is convenient or because it offers a training opportunity. In more rural areas, competitors are up in the wee hours to drive to distant trials. Remember when I talked about the addictive nature of agility?

In this section, I highlight a variety of intermediate skills that you will find useful at trials. You will find key strategies for memorizing courses, ideas for managing your nerves, and a plan for what to do when things go wrong on course. Let's get started.

Part VI
On the Agility Circuit

25 Fail-Safe Strategies for Memorizing Courses

I came close to quitting agility only once in more than 14 years of competing. I was running my new dog, who was much faster than my first. We were flying along when all of a sudden, my mind was literally a blank. I slammed to a halt and stood helpless in the middle of the ring. My dog stopped and barked at me in annoyance. I was terrifically embarrassed. My confidence was shaken. After this event, I began to worry about getting lost before each run, and sure enough, it happened again. I knew that I had to change the pattern so that my anxiety would not bleed the pleasure out of agility. I began to talk to friends and other competitors about how they memorized standard and jumpers courses. The result was that I acquired a series of techniques that I now use and share with students.

For some folks, memorizing courses comes easily. You may not need all of the steps I describe here. But for others, like me, learning complex courses is more difficult, and the methodical process I describe will definitely help. It does get easier over time and when you have a plan. The bottom line is that it's impossible to pay adequate attention to your dog on course if you are wondering where to go.

Prior to Walking the Course
The hardest part of memorization happens before you set foot on a course. These strategies work well for standard or jumpers courses.
1. On the map provided by the judge, use a pencil to draw a line from obstacle to obstacle like those connect-the-dot pictures we did as youngsters. Draw the line as your dog would run, rather than as a straight line.
2. Trace the general flow of the obstacles several times. Often it is easier to memorize something if we physically engage part of our body during the process. This is called kinesthetic learning. Repeat this until you can trace the flow quickly and smoothly.
3. Trace the general flow again on your palm or on the ground.

Draw a line from obstacle to obstacle.

4. Memorize the order of the specific obstacles.
5. Close your eyes and say all of the obstacles in order without peeking. This is critical. Because you need to watch your dog during the run, you must know what is coming next without looking.
6. Have a friend quiz you. Say the obstacles in order as fast as you will need to run them.
7. Now return to your map. Identify the places on course that will require more direction from you, such as discriminations and changes of direction. Place a mark on your map to note where you will position yourself to handle the challenge.

After this effort, you will start your walk-through ready to concentrate on details rather than hoping that you can learn the course in time.

Maximizing Your Walk-Through

Once you can get on the course, do the following:
1. Walk the whole thing a couple of times to check that the flow matches what you saw on the map. If something looks dramatically different, note that.
2. Next, divide up the course in your mind. For most intermediate-level courses, I split the course into thirds. There are generally very natural "breaking points," like a sharp turn or the table

On the Agility Circuit

or a cross that changes the direction. Now I have three short courses to learn. If I start to get nervous, I ask myself, "Could I remember six or seven obstacles in class?" The answer is always yes.

3. Now I literally memorize them as three short exercises. While I am walking, I even say to myself "New course" when I hit the next section. This strategy is particularly important on jumpers courses where there are so few landmarks to help you find your way.

4. Once you know the course, concentrate on the details of your handling. In congested areas, get down to your dog's eye level to see what he will see. You may observe a turn while he sees an inviting tunnel. Strategize how you will position yourself to help him go in the right direction. Where will your feet be pointing? What will your arms be doing? What words will you be using?

5. If there is a particular place that you tend to get lost, practice that section with extra intensity. For example, when I got lost, it was often after I had sent my dog into a tunnel. Go figure. Now I pay special attention to what obstacle follows each tunnel. I also do extra practice at places where I know I will need to look down at my dog and then back up at the course because it is easy to get disoriented in those spots.

6. Before the end of the walk-through, run the course with your invisible dog. Your goal is to move quickly without having to think too much. Make sure to include all of your strategies and exact command words. Also, make sure that you can find the next obstacle without looking up to check because this often causes dogs to do the unexpected. Use all the time until the judge asks you to clear the course.

Memorizing Two Courses at Once
Sometimes you may find yourself competing at two different levels in the same venue. For example, you might be entered in Novice Jumpers and Open Standard. Occasionally, this means that you will need to memorize two courses at once. When this situation arises, memorize and walk the course you will run first. Then mentally set it aside. Walk and memorize the other course. Then return to the first and get a quick last walk if there is time, or watch several other teams to refresh your memory.

After Your Walk-Through

For many folks, the previous steps are plenty of preparation. For me, I add four additional powerful memorization strategies that I have adapted from a book *Agility Success,* by Angelica Steinker, an expert in the mental aspect of agility competition.

1. Picture a blimp flying over the ring with someone taking a video of you running the course from the air. Picture yourself running through the course and smoothly negotiating all of the turns and changes of direction.

2. Picture yourself running the course at twice the normal speed. If you can do this from start to finish, it will make your real run seem like you have all the time in the world.

Fail-Safe Strategies for Memorizing Courses

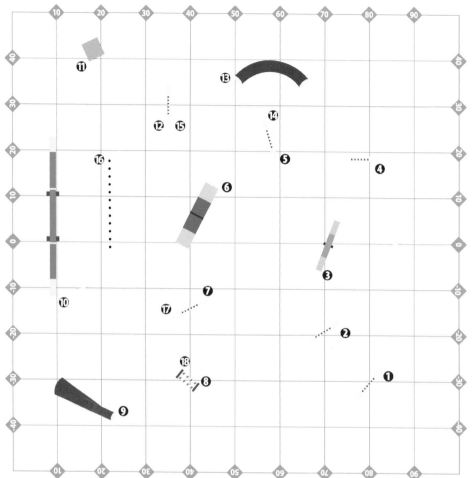

Figure 25.1

3. Imagine yourself running the course while you hum a song you particularly like. Okay, I know this sounds really strange, but music puts you into a different part of your brain where memorization comes easily.

4. Pretend that you are watching yourself on television. See yourself run the whole course exactly as you will run it. Of course, imagine lots of applause at the end. This is my favorite part—I love that applause.

On the Agility Circuit

Mental Practice

For practice, I have made up an intermediate standard course, which is shown in Figure 25.1. Your job is to memorize it. Utilize the seven steps suggested earlier prior to your run.

Did you remember to divide the course into thirds? For me, this course has a natural break at the end of the A-frame and after tunnel #13. It might be different for you.

Now let's see how well you memorized. Close your eyes and say the course as fast as you can. Have a friend follow along on the map to check that you have it right. If you nailed it, you would be ready to use your walk-through to maximum advantage.

But your work isn't over. Now pick one or more of the other strategies and practice using them. Visualize yourself from the air or on television while you run the course. Imagine running it at twice your normal speed or while you hum. Don't you love all that clapping when you cross the finish line?

Concluding Thoughts

Two last notes. First, I still get a blank moment occasionally on course, although they are thankfully few and far between. When it happens, I have tried to teach myself to keep moving forward rather than stopping and spinning in a circle. In most cases, the next obvious obstacle is the correct one. Once my dog takes it, the whole picture snaps back into place.

Second, students ask me if memorizing ever gets easier. The answer is a resounding yes. It seems that at a certain point, new connections are made in the brain and then this job is not as arduous. I think you can accelerate the process by making a habit of memorizing courses that you gather at trials or find in magazines. Find a map right now and get to work!

26 Video Is Your Friend

A number of years ago, when my Sheltie, Scout, was relatively new to the sport, she and I were working our way through a standard course. Things were going nicely until we reached the table. Although she had had some early issues with the table—why would I get on that thing and *stop*?—she appeared to be solid with this obstacle at the time of the trial. However, during our run, she glanced at the table but tore by and dove into a nearby tunnel. I had no idea what had gone wrong.

Fortunately, a friend had videotaped the run. When she handed me the camera, she chuckled. When I looked at the tape, I knew why she was amused. Rather than standing by the table quietly and giving Scout clear physical and verbal cues, I had started to dance. It looked a bit like a tap dance routine in an old musical. Clearly, I had communicated to her that we were continuing to move forward. The tunnel was simply a natural place to go next.

Since that day, I have become a true believer in the power of video to improve handling skills. Capturing your run on tape can help you see what you did, rather than what you think you did, and assist you in analyzing what would work better. On the second day of the trial at which I had done my dance routine, I planted myself firmly by the table and kept my feet on the ground. Lo and behold, my good girl charged onto the table and dropped like a rock.

Focus on One Thing at a Time
It is easy to fall into the habit of merely striving to get through each run in class or at a trial. You will improve more quickly if you focus on one specific thing you would like to improve each time you run. For example, you might want to work on your speed changes or using a timely false turn. Video is a powerful tool for providing feedback on whether you executed the skill exactly as you wanted.

Video can be done professionally.

Who Can Record a Run?

Video can be done professionally or by a friend and in class or at trials. Just this week, one my students brought her camera and computer to class. After each sequence, students gathered around to analyze their handling. Then they reran the same sequence to fix any mistakes they might have made. Even the small viewing screen on video cameras can provide immediate and impartial feedback. At trials, professional videotaping is sometimes available for a reasonable price.

Common Video-Captured Mistakes

In a single class, we were able to isolate these common mistakes using the video feedback:

- One handler ran an entire sequence with her arms at shoulder height even though she wanted the dog to take several obstacles that were quite close. The result was that the dog ran around several obstacles because the raised arm was a cue to work laterally. The handler successfully reran the sequence, remembering to drop her arm when she wanted the dog to come in tightly.
- Another handler wanted her dog to take a jump straight ahead while she slid laterally to execute a front cross. However, the dog followed her movement and missed the jump. The video showed that she pulled her arm in too quickly before the dog had committed to the

jump. When she reran with her arm fully extended, the dog read the cue easily and took the jump while the handler got in position to front cross.

- A third handler was able to see why her dog kept taking the A-frame rather than the tunnel, which was set underneath in a tight discrimination. Rather than driving the line to the tunnel and holding on until the dog committed, the video captured her moving one of her feet off to the side in the direction she would be going after the tunnel. This was just enough to miscue her dog and send him up the contact. She reran, held steady at the tunnel, and bingo.

Take Note
We often get so excited when we compete that we exit the ring unable to remember exactly how we handled certain sections. Video bridges the gaps in our memory and helps us improve our skills.

I can't say that I always enjoy watching the tapes. I prefer my mental image of myself floating through every course perfectly synchronized with my dog. I often creep off to the DVD player in the bedroom to play the video in private if a run has not gone as planned. After I watch, I mentally practice how I should have handled a difficult section. On the other hand, I save videos of good runs for years. I resist the urge to show them to dinner guests, but it takes considerable self-control.

Concluding Thoughts

I have come to think of video as a good friend that specializes in immediate, untarnished feedback. Sometimes what I see makes me happy. Sometimes it makes me cringe. But I know that the feedback from video and my teacher are my best hope for continuous improvement.

Video Is Your Friend

27

Managing Ring Nerves

Because you have arrived at Chapter 27 of an intermediate agility book, the odds are good that you enjoy the process of training. It is also possible that trialing is a different matter. It is not uncommon for handlers to feel a flood of anxiety when placed in a competitive situation. For some folks, ring nerves simply fade away over time, but for others, trials remain stressful.

At every trial, we would not have to interview too many folks before someone would describe her emotions like this:

I look forward to my agility class every week, but on trial day, I feel anxious as soon as I get up. All day long, I'm nervous. I often have trouble memorizing the course from the map. I start remembering the last trial where I got lost and felt embarrassed. I begin to imagine that happening again.

When I finally see the ring being set for my class, I feel intense butterflies in my stomach. By the time I'm ringside with my dog waiting to run, my heart is pounding and I'm hyperventilating. I've felt quite dizzy several times. There have also been times when I've directed my dog over several obstacles and then my mind turned blank. I had no idea where to go.

Naturally, these kinds of feelings lead to serious thoughts of dropping out of trials. Folks start agility to have fun with their dogs, and fear isn't part of that plan. If this sounds anything like your experience, there are strategies to help you relax. They are tried and true by generations of professional and recreational athletes. They take time and energy, but they work. They worked for a number of my students, and they have certainly helped me.

If you are anxious, you may have found that friends will offer all sorts of advice. Some will tell you that you need to change your goal from qualifying to just having fun. They will suggest that

Dogs exhibit stress on course in a variety of ways, including by slowing down.

you need to prepare more for your runs. They will imply that you can calm down if you just try harder. It is all well intended. The problem is that it won't work if you are in a panic.

Let's take a look at what causes some of us to become fearful. Then we can look at a fix.

Management Techniques

Diane Peters Mayer, M.S.W, is a psychotherapist and a performance anxiety coach. She has worked with many agility competitors and written a comprehensive book on the subject (*Conquering Ring Nerves*, Wiley, 2004). Diane writes:

"Some people see competing as perilous in an unnamed way. We know an agility trial isn't physically dangerous, but emotionally it is. Who knows what might happen in the ring? You might forget the course, fail to qualify, or humiliate yourself in front of your peers. The brain does not know the difference between a real or perceived threat. It does its job of protecting you by sending out messages that you must fight or flee. Hormones flood your body and cause your heart to beat faster, your muscles to tense, your stomach to tense, and your breathing to become shallow. All this happens in a split second without conscious thought."

What Diane highlights is that an intellectual effort will not overcome performance anxiety. She writes, "The one strategy that can override these distressing symptoms is breathing. Breathing

Dog Anxiety
Dogs get anxious too. Sometimes they are picking up on your nerves, and other times they bring issues of their own. They exhibit stress in a variety of ways that include racing around, sniffing, yawning, and slowing down. If your dog shows any of these behaviors, take a break from the situation that is triggering the anxiety. Use your problem solving to make a plan to help your pup relax and enjoy the game.

operates on both an unconscious and conscious level because we can control its frequency, depth, and length. When we slow and lengthen the breath, we calm both the mind and the body. Breathing activates the part of the nervous system where the relaxation response resides."

Breathing
Learning to control your breathing is a relatively simple process. Start at home when you are quiet and relaxed. Diane suggests that you follow these steps:
1. Get a timer and set it for two minutes.
2. Get comfortably seated in a chair and close your eyes. Keep your feet flat and your hands in your lap.
3. Take slow, deep breaths through your nose only. Make sure that each breath is long and even.
4. When the timer goes off, take a moment to return to your normal breathing. Evaluate how you are feeling.
  Practice daily, and gradually increase the time to five minutes.

Hit the Road
Once you are comfortable with the breathing process, it is time to take it out of the house. Your goal is to put the technique into action while you are standing up and with your eyes open. You don't need to be stressed in any way. Remember to keep your breaths slow and deep. Practice in line at the supermarket with your eyes open. Practice at your training class. Go to a trial that you haven't entered and practice at ringside.

When you decide that you are ready to enter a trial, use your ability to control your breathing throughout the day. Diane suggests that you use your controlled breathing in the following places:
- as soon as you pop out of bed in the wee hours
- on the road to the show
- in the parking lot at the trial
- while you are doing your walk-through
- while you are waiting to run
- as you put your dog in a *stay* and lead out on course

When I began to practice this technique at trials, I found that I did fine until I was waiting my turn to go into the ring. As I watched the teams ahead of me run, I started to worry about remembering the course, and my breathing went into high gear. To help myself at that juncture, I began to combine breathing with a second technique.

Picture Success

In Chapter 25, I suggested that it may help you learn courses if you visualize yourself running the course smoothly and successfully. This exercise has an additional benefit of helping calm frazzled nerves.

Take Note
Willpower is not enough to drive fear away. In fact, trying to tough it out is likely to increase your stress.

While I was waiting to run, I stopped watching the dogs ahead of me. Rather, I crouched or sat down with my dog and pictured every detail of my perfect run while controlling my breathing. I sang my pup a short song—it's difficult to hyperventilate while singing. Even as I moved up to the gate, I concentrated on my breathing and smiled at my dog. It worked. I was in control and ready to go.

All top performers at every level of sports are experts at visualization. An Olympic skater rehearses her perfect performance hundreds of times before competition. Tiger Woods imagines himself hitting the perfect drive with the perfect form while relaxed and focused. Interestingly, mental practice has proven to be as effective in improving performance as actual practice is.

Diane recommends that you practice guided imagery as you did your breathing, starting at home in a quiet environment. As you did before, sit in a comfortable, quiet place. Start with your

Visualizing your run may help calm your nerves.

On the Agility Circuit

It may help you learn a course if you can visualize you and your dog running it smoothly.

breathing practice. While you continue to take slow, deep breaths, picture an agility course. See all the details of your perfect run. See yourself as relaxed, confident, and energized. Imagine yourself feeling successful after the run.

   As you did with your breathing, regularly practice the skill of visualization. Over time, you will find that you can feel the grass under your feet and feel the morning chill in the air while imagining your run in great detail.

Concluding Thoughts

Ring nerves won't go away overnight. It takes practice, time, and determination to reduce performance anxiety. But if you want to compete at your peak and have more fun, you can retrain yourself. Have patience. Be kind to yourself.

28
Utilizing the Warm-Up Jump

I admit it. I spy at agility trials. I covertly watch competitors' behavior during the day, which keeps me out of trouble between runs. In recent months, my observations have focused on what handlers do before their runs. It was my hypothesis that most handlers don't have a regular routine for getting their dog warmed up and focused in preparation for a run at a trial. One of the most important aspects of a pre-run routine is using the warm-up jump that is strategically provided near each ring. However, I had my suspicions that the majority of competitors didn't use this jump at all, or they used it casually, without a clear plan, to jump their dog once or twice. My undercover observations confirmed this.

Once I knew this to be true, I interviewed a number of folks at several trials. In response to my question of why they skipped any use of the warm-up jump, they provided the following reasons most often:

- They were worried about other parts of their upcoming run, such as contacts or weaves, and jumping was the last thing on their mind.
- They wanted to spend every possible minute memorizing their course.
- The jump was out of sight and out of mind.
- They got their dog out too late and ran out of time to include jumping.

One of the most important aspects of a pre-run routine is using the warm-up jump.

Here is a sobering thought: Standard agility courses consist of 80 percent jumps and tunnels. Ignoring an opportunity to practice this skill is a strategic mistake. If you want your dog to compete at his peak, thoughtful use of the warm-up jump is one of the most important aspects of getting ready to run.

Let's take a look at how you can use the jump to prepare your dog for what to expect on your course. Keep in mind that you shouldn't train new behaviors at the jump. Rather, practice known behaviors that you will be putting into action.

Start During Your Walk-Through

When you are in the ring memorizing your course, take note of any specific issues that may come up related to jumps. Here are some challenges you may face:

- Is the first obstacle a jump that requires a lead out?
- Will your dog be taking any of the jumps at sharp angles?
- Will you be doing a rear cross or front cross near a jump?
- Are there any places where your dog will have to go over a jump and then wrap around the outside of the stanchion with a front cross?
- Are you going to be in a position where your dog will have to jump at some distance from you? Once you know what your dog will encounter, you can make a plan for the warm-up jump.

Practice Jumps
If you have not yet purchased any equipment, start today with jumps. There are a full range of jumps, from inexpensive PVC jumps to trial-quality metal jumps. You can teach dozens of skills using one jump, and three can keep you busy for months.

Maximize Your Use of the Jump

Remember to get your dog out early enough to potty and do a general warm-up. Then head to the jump. Ideally, you will be there within ten minutes of running. Start by simply jumping your pup to warm him up. First, I run with my dog a couple of times and then send him over the jump a couple of times. If I am far enough from the ring so that it is legal, I toss his toy as he jumps or play a game of tug after he jumps because it gets him fired up. Then I ask him to do at least one figure eight over the jump. It is my goal to get his muscles warm and to get him as excited as possible. Next I get strategic:

- If I am going to do a lead out onto the course, I put my dog on a *stay* and lead out. I alternate calling him over and reinforcing with a treat or tossing a cookie backward to reward him for staying.
- If I am going to encounter some jumps at a sharp angle, I start at the same angle and run with him while he takes the jump.
- If I am going to perform a front cross or rear cross, I practice either or both. Again, I reinforce with either a cookie or a toss of the toy and a game of tug.

On the Agility Circuit

- If I am going to need to wrap him around the stanchion to switch direction or to pull him between two obstacles, I send him over the jump and get as tight a turn with him as I can.
- If I am going to need some distance work, I finish my jumping routine by putting my dog on a *stay* and standing off to the side. I send him over the jump. After I reward him, I back up once or twice until I am working at the distance I will need him to perform from in the ring.

Start by simply jumping your dog to warm him up.

Any time your dog gives you the exact behavior that you want while warming up, throw a party with small treats or a good game. This entire process takes two or three minutes, which gives you plenty of time to get to your ring within five dogs of your turn.

Warm-Up Jump Etiquette

As with other aspects of agility, there are clear rules about how to use the warm-up jump appropriately and avoid annoying others. First and foremost, always give priority to those teams that are just about to go into the ring. If a crowd is waiting for the jump, then limit your time on the jump to four or five times over it, emphasizing a different skill each time. If time allows, you can always go back to it when others have had their turn.

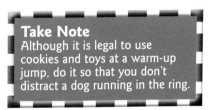

Take Note
Although it is legal to use cookies and toys at a warm-up jump, do it so that you don't distract a dog running in the ring.

If there is some skill that your dog struggles with during your warm-up, the practice jump is not the right place to teach it. Just file the information away for training when you get home. In the meantime, figure out another way to handle the challenge on your upcoming run. For example, if you had hoped to lead out but your dog is just too excited, you should change plans to run with him and work on proofing your *stay* before the next trial.

If your dog has any aggression or possessiveness issues, be attentive around the jump because there are often other dogs close by. There is often heavy walking traffic in the jump area too.

Concluding Thoughts

It is not chance that all trials provide a warm-up jump rather than a warm-up tunnel or warm-up weaves. Efficient, lively jumping is the basis of all agility. If you want a peak performance, take advantage of the opportunity the jump provides you to get your dog ready.

29
Record Keeping

There are more agility organizations than you can count on one hand. Each offers myriad titles that your dog can earn (with your help, of course). Although it is not as exciting as a great run, it is essential that you keep good records of trial results so that you know what you have earned, when you can move up to the next level, and when to be ecstatically happy about a notable benchmark in your agility career. Without good record keeping, you will quickly lose track of where your dog is on the path to earning an OAJ, C-ATCH, or CL2-F.

A dog's records are posted on the organizations' websites. Sometimes this service is free, and sometimes you must pay extra to access them. In every case, the process of posting trial results is slow, so you may not be able to find information when you need it. This makes keeping good records yourself a fine idea.

I think of record keepers as falling into one of three groups:
- the detail folks
- the organized crowd
- the barely-holding-it-together people

I will describe each of these approaches. In the Appendix, you will find a form approach for each style.

The Detail Folks

This group thrives on information. Their record keeping is an art form. They record every detail, no matter how small, about every run. They record information about dogs other than their own. They plug in mathematical formulas to determine their dogs' speed.

Without seeing their record books, you can identify this group at a glance. They wear ironed clothes to agility trials. They pack and unpack their agility accoutrements, all color-coordinated, with precision. Many unroll carpets in their tents and set up tables. On hot days, they rig up water misters to keep their tenting area cool. The rest of us crowd in. At home, I suspect that they alphabetize their spices.

The seriously anal keep the following:

- trial date
- organization (AKC, CPE, NADAC, USDAA, etc.)
- name of the show (often the name of the club putting on the show)
- location
- field conditions
- weather
- class (such as Standard or Pairs)
- number of dogs in the class
- level (such as Level 1 or Advanced)
- jump height
- judge
- whether the dog qualified in the class
- time for the dog
- placement
- standard course time (set mathematically by the judge)
- course yardage (announced by the judge)
- dog's yards per second (course yardage divided by a dog's time)
- number of dogs that qualified
- name, breed, and running time for the first through fourth place finishers
- additional information (such as speed points, double Qs)

If you count yourself in this group, you will like Form 1 in the Appendix.

The Organized Crowd

This group loves a sense of order. They never have to go to the American Kennel Club (AKC) or United States Dog Agility Association (USDAA) websites to find out if their dog earned their Open Agility Jumpers or Masters Agility Dog titles. They know the minute it happens. At trials, their setups are spit and polish. Shade cloths are fastened perfectly. The cooler, always filled with organic dog treats and snacks, is always in the same corner. At home, these are folks who fold their undies and socks.

At trials, the organized crowd differs from the anal detail crowd in two significant ways. While their tents are very neat, they do not haul along enough furniture to require an interior decorator. Second, the organized limit their record keeping to details about their dog only, rather than recording details about dogs who beat them and whom they may not even know.

This group keeps the following information:

- trial date
- organization (AKC, CPE, NADAC, USDAA, etc.)
- name of the show (often the name of the club putting it on)
- location
- field conditions
- class (such as Standard or Pairs)
- level (such as Level 1 or Advanced)
- jump height
- number of dogs in the class
- judge
- whether the dog qualified in each class
- whether the dog placed
- time for the dog
- additional information (such as speed points or double Qs)

If this is your style, use Form 2 in the Appendix for your record keeping.

On the Agility Circuit

Questioning Your Score
If you ever have a question about your score at a trial run, it is important to talk to the judge as soon as possible without interrupting a class. Remember that the judge will see hundreds of runs during a day. However, like baseball umpires, judges rarely change a "call" after the fact. Keep in mind that you will get to try again the next day or week.

The Barely-Holding-It-Together People

These folks live on the edge. They struggle to manage their agility calendar: Hey, did I ever send my entry for that trial? When they send it, they forget to enclose a check. Now and then, they show up at trials they never entered. (Okay, I admit it. I did do this once, but it was years ago.)

When packing for an agility trial, they stuff their agility supplies anywhere they will fit in the car. At a trial, the shade cloth sides on their canopy flap in the wind, the dog treats are still in the fridge at home, and their chair disappeared at an event last weekend. At home, their ribbons are tossed into a drawer that is next to the drawer where every sort of undergarment lives in a heap.

This group maintains minimal information. They must occasionally check with an agility organization to confirm that they really do have two legs toward their Gamblers title. Although they may construct or purchase a record-keeping book, their information is never written on the lines. It includes:

- trial date
- organization (AKC, CPE, NADAC, USDAA, etc.)
- name of the show (often the name of the club putting it on)
- location
- class
- level
- judge
- whether the dog qualified in each class
- whether the dog placed
- additional information (such as speed points or double Qs)

If you are in this group (be honest), use Form 3. Your goal is to simply write on the lines and fill in every blank.

Concluding Thoughts

Although you can purchase premade record books, it may suit you better to make up a template that includes exactly what you want. The bottom line is that whatever your style, keep track as best you can. Don't count on your memory.

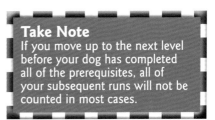

Take Note
If you move up to the next level before your dog has completed all of the prerequisites, all of your subsequent runs will not be counted in most cases.

hope that my passion for this sport has come through as I have shared my thoughts in this book. My dream is that you and your dog will build your relationship over many years through this sport.

Since I wrote my first agility book, newer competitors have occasionally found me at trials and told me that they found it useful. This has given me great pleasure. I hope that you find this book equally useful. I like the idea that when you finish with this one, it is dirty and filled with notes about your training sessions and what you have learned about handling or about your dog.

As your skills grow, you will undoubtedly attend a variety of classes and seminars. You may even choose to spend your vacation at an agility camp. Try new things. Build a range of skills. Beware of absolutes—there is no single right way to train your dog. For example, interactive toy play such as tugging has become a fad in agility. While tugging is a wonderful way to keep a dog energized and reinforce a desired behavior, many great teams have been trained without toys. As long as you are a good trainer, a rewarding partner, and an effective problem solver, you can work around most issues. The one exception to this is aggression. If you have a dog about whom you have any doubts, make the courageous decision to try another sport that your dog can do on leash.

As I have written these chapters, I am often aware that there is a missing voice. I wonder what our dogs would tell us about the agility game if they could talk. At the risk of some serious personification, I offer my best estimation of what they might want us to know:

- I like it when you keep training simple and fun.
- I don't like to show pain, but I tell you, nonetheless, when I am hurt. If I slow down, creep down the contacts, refuse a familiar obstacle, stutter-step before any obstacle, or just seem "off," I hope that you will be a good listener and help me feel better.
- It makes me anxious when you expect me to do things in trials that I haven't mastered in practice. Whenever you use the phrase "I'll see what happens," I know that we're in trouble.
- I appreciate it when you gently reteach me something I have forgotten. I don't mean to forget, but sometimes I do. You forget things too. I forgive you.
- I like it when we take a mental and physical break from agility. It is the best when we go for a hike in the woods, play flying disc, or throw a ball. I promise that I will come back to agility performing better than before I left.
- Remember that no matter what happens at a trial, you and I are going home together. I like it when we climb in the car together at the end of the day, tired and happy. I am a lucky dog.

I fully believe that dogs share these thoughts with us in subtle ways through their behavior and body language. Think back to that day when you arrived at your first agility class with the intent of having fun with your dog. As you improve your skills, remember to keep this goal at the center of your ambitions.

I look forward to meeting you and your good dog somewhere on the agility circuit.

Appendix I

Key to Obstacles

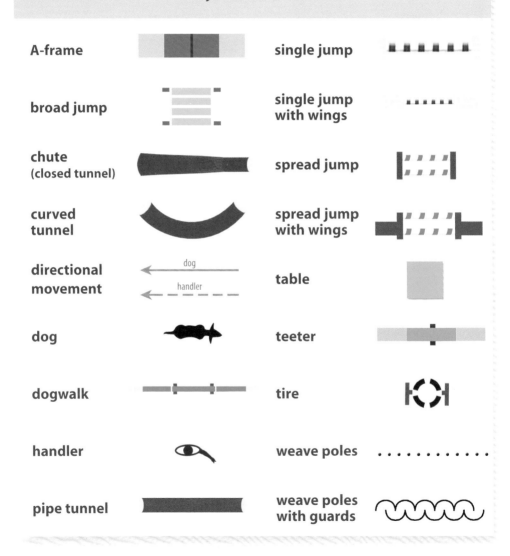

A-frame		single jump	
broad jump		single jump with wings	
chute (closed tunnel)		spread jump	
curved tunnel		spread jump with wings	
directional movement	dog / handler	table	
dog		teeter	
dogwalk		tire	
handler		weave poles	
pipe tunnel		weave poles with guards	

Form 1

Trial Date _____

Organization

AAC_____ AKC _____ ASCA _____ CKC_____ CPE_____

DOCNA_____ NADAC_____ TDAA _____ USDAA_____ Other _____

Name of Show_____

Location _____

Field Conditions _____

Weather _____

Class _____

Number of Dogs in the Class _____

Level _____

Jump Height _____

Judge _____

Qualified _____**Did not Qualify** _____ **Time** _____

Placement _____

Standard Course Time _____**Course Yardage**_____

Yards per Second _____

Number of Dogs That Qualified _____

Overall Placements

First Place _____ Time _____Breed _____

Second Place _____ Time _____Breed _____

Third Place _____ Time _____Breed _____

Fourth Place _____ Time _____Breed _____

Additional Information _____

_____

_____

_____

Form 2

Trial Date _____

Organization

AAC_____ AKC _____ ASCA _____ CKC_____ CPE _____

DOCNA_____ NADAC_____ TDAA _____ USDAA_____ Other _____

Name of Show _____

Location _____

Field Conditions _____

Class _____

Number of Dogs in the Class _____

Level _____ _____

Jump Height _____

Number of Dogs in the Class _____

Judge _____

Qualified _____ **Did not Qualify**_____ **Time** _____

Placement _____

Additional Information _____

_____

_____

_____

_____

_____

_____

_____

_____

_____

The Intermediate's Guide to Dog Agility

Form 3

Trial Date _____

Organization

AAC_____ AKC _____ ASCA _____ CKC_____ CPE_____

DOCNA_____ NADAC_____ TDAA _____ USDAA_____ Other _____

Name of Show_____

Location _____

Class _____

Level _____

Judge _____

Qualified _____ **Did not Qualify**_____ **Time** _____

Placement _____

Additional Information _____

_____

_____

_____

_____

_____

_____

_____

_____

_____

_____

_____

_____

_____

Appendix II

Resources

Organizations

Agility Association of Canada (AAC)
www.aac.ca

American Kennel Club (AKC)
Telephone: (919) 816-3725, (919) 816-3559
Fax: (919) 816-4204
E-Mail: agility@akc.org
www.akc.org

Australian Shepherd Club of America (ASCA)
Telephone: (979) 778-1082
Fax: (979) 778-1898
E-Mail: agility@asca.org
www.asca.org

Canadian Kennel Club (CKC)
Telephone: (416) 675-5511
E-Mail: information@ckc.ca
www.ckc.ca

Canine Performance Events, Inc. (CPE)
E-Mail: cpe@charter.net
www.k9cpe.com

Dogs on Course in North America (DOCNA)
Fax: (602) 375-0385
E-Mail: info@docna.com
www.docna.com

Teacup Dogs Agility Association (TDAA)
Telephone: (217) 521-7955
www.k9tdaa.com

The Kennel Club
Telephone: 0870 606 6750
Fax: 020 7518 1058
www.the-kennel-club.org.uk

Northern American Dog Agility Council (NADAC)
E-Mail: info@nadac.com
www.nadac.com

United Kennel Club (UKC)
Telephone: (269) 343-9020
Fax: (269) 343-7037
E-Mail: mmorgan@ukcdogs.com
www.ukcdogs.com

United States Dog Agility Association (USDAA)
Telephone: (972) 487-2200
Fax: (972) 231-9700
www.usdaa.com

Books

Mayer, Diane Peters.
Conquering Ring Nerves: A Step-by-Step Program for all Dog Sports.
Hoboken: Wiley. 2004.

Steinker, Angelica.
Agility Success. 2000.

DVDs

Ann Croft:
4 on the Floor: Modified Running Contacts

Greg Derrett:
Agility Foundation Training
Great Dog...Shame About the Handler!
The Winning Combination
On Course to Excel

Susan Garrett:
2 x 2 Weave Training
Success With One Jump

Susan Salo:
Foundation Jumping

Rachel Sanders:
The Pre-Sports Puppy

Magazines

Clean Run Magazine
Clean Run Productions, LLC
17 Industrial Dr.
South Hadley, MA 01075
Telephone: (800) 311-6503
E-Mail: info@cleanrun.com
www.cleanrun.com

Dog Sport Magazine
PO Box 189
Amsterdam, NY 12010 USA
Telephone: 1-866-DOG-SPRT (364-7778)
E-Mail: custserv@ntiglobal.com
www.dogsportmagazine.com

Supplies

Affordable Agility
www.affordableagility.com

Doggone Good!
www.doggonegood.com

J & J Dog Supplies
www.jjdog.com

Websites

www.awesomepaws.us
www.cleanrun.com
www.clickerdogs.com
www.clickertraining.com
www.gtagility.com
www.jumpdogs.com
www.lotp.com
www.nylabone.com
www.tfh.com

Index

Numbers

2 x 2 method, 125
90-degree turn, 53–59
180-degree turns
    about, 81–82
    common issues, 88
    mental practice, 88–89
    practice sequences, 161–162
    prerequisite skills, 82
    sequences with wide turns, 88
    teaching, 82–85
270-degree turns
    about, 81–82
    common issues, 88
    mental practice, 88–89
    practice sequences, 163
    prerequisite skills, 82
    sequences with wide turns, 88
    teaching, 85–87

A

AAC (Agility Association of Canada), 244
abandoning your dog, 181–182
acceleration
    body language for, 46
    teaching, 47–48

Affordable Agility website, 245

Agility Association of Canada (AAC), 244
agility circuit
    managing ring nerves, 225–229
    memorizing courses, 215–219
    questioning your score, 237
    record keeping, 235–237, 241–243
    reinforcing contacts, 190–191
    reinforcing stay, 202–203
    as training, 193
    using videos, 221–223
    warm-up jumps, 231–233
agility courses. *See* courses
agility maps, reading, 11
agility skills checklist, 25–31
agility, sport of
    beginner versus intermediate levels, 11–14,
      174
    keeping it fun for your dog, 17–21
    test for being hooked on, 8
AKC (American Kennel Club)
    competition classes, 15
    contact information, 244
    on qualifying scores, 13–15
    record keeping and, 236
    on repositioning dogs, 202
American Kennel Club (AKC)
    competition classes, 15
    contact information, 244
    on qualifying scores, 13–15
    record keeping and, 236
    on repositioning dogs, 202
angles, teaching, 134–136

The Intermediate's Guide to Dog Agility

anxiety
    changing pattern of, 215
    conveying, 185
    in dogs, 226–227
    managing, 225–229
ASCA (Australian Shepherd Club of America),
        15, 244
Australian Shepherd Club of America (ASCA),
        15, 244

B

backchaining
    about, 149–150
    clusters of obstacles, 152–153
    obstacle by obstacle, 151–152
    practice sequences, 159–166
bars, knocking, 208–209
beginner agility
    agility skills checklist, 25–31
    foundation skills checklist, 23–25
    intermediate versus, 11–14, 174
    self-consciousness and, 141
    transitioning from, 14–15
behavior
    de-motivating, 180–185
    inherent in breeds, 146
    motivational issues, 179–185
    recapturing lost contacts, 187–195
    reinforcing, 33
    synchronizing, 189
blame, avoiding, 17, 21
blocking obstacles, 132
body language
    for acceleration, 46
    checking, 59
    for deceleration, 46
    dogs' ability to read, 17
    self-consciousness about, 141
    teaching changes, 46–51

breathing, controlling, 227–229
bridges for obstacles, 208

C

Canadian Kennel Club (CKC), 244
Canine Performance Events (CPE)
    competition classes, 14–15
    contact information, 244
    record keeping and, 236
    style and atmosphere of, 212
challenges. See also problem-solving
    alternating with easy games, 18
    beginner versus intermediate levels, 12–13,
        174
    common, 145–146
    identifying, 143, 145–147
    individual, 145
    intermediate course examples, 171–175
    mental practice, 146–147
    start line, 132–134
changing speeds
    about, 43–46
    common issues, 51
    mental practice, 51
    practice sequences, 160, 163–164
    prerequisite skills, 43
    teaching acceleration, 46–48
    teaching body language changes, 46
    teaching deceleration, 46, 48–51
CKC (Canadian Kennel Club), 244
Clean Run Magazine, 194, 245
clickers
    as reward system, 19–20

Index

training with, 23
collection, 45
commands
    heel, 23, 27, 191
    recall, 23
    stay, 23, 29, 197–203
    verbal, 117, 143
competition classes, 14–15
contact obstacles. *See* obstacles
contacts, lost, 187–195
contact zones
    contact obstacles and, 27–28
    running through, 189
cookie delivery, 33, 181
courses
    beginner versus intermediate-level, 11–14, 174
    getting started on, 131–137
    intermediate, 169–175
    memorizing, 215–219
CPE (Canine Performance Events)
    competition classes, 14–15
    contact information, 244
    record keeping and, 236
    style and atmosphere of, 212
Croft, Ann, 194, 244
curves
    obstacles on, 25–26
    running outside of, 56

D

deceleration
    body language for, 46
    to complete standstill, 50
    teaching, 48–51
    teaching front cross, 64
de-motivating behavior
    abandoning your dog, 181–182
    accepting slow performances, 183–184
    asking for too much, 182–183
    conveying anxiety, 185
    delaying rewards, 184–185
    excessive practice, 185
    forgetting play, 183
    reacting negatively, 180–181
    reward predictability as, 183
Derrett, Greg
    DVDs by, 244
    handling rear cross, 71
    high-tech front cross, 61
    website for, 4
de-stick game, 192–193
discouragement, avoiding, 18–19
discriminations
    common issues, 112
    intermediate course example, 169–170
    mental practice, 112–113
    practice sequences, 164, 166
    prerequisite skills, 107–108
    teaching handling options, 108–112
DOCNA (Dogs on Course in North America)
    competition classes, 15
    contact information, 244
    on repositioning dogs, 202
Doggone Good! website, 245
Dogs on Course in North America (DOCNA)
    competition classes, 15
    contact information, 244
    on repositioning dogs, 202
Dog Sport Magazine, 46, 245

The Intermediate's Guide to Dog Agility

dogwalk, 207–208
driving ahead, 26–27
driving the line
    common issues, 96–97
    mental practice, 97
    practice sequences, 158, 161, 165–166
    prerequisite skills, 92–93
    pushing versus, 91–92
    teaching, 93–96

E

exercise
    adjusting to dog's needs, 185
    practicing excessively, 185
eye contact, 58, 66

F

false turns
    about, 99–100
    common issues, 104
    locating, 100–101
    mental practice, 105
    practice sequences, 162, 166
    prerequisite skills, 100
    teaching, 101–104
fear (ring nerves), 225–229
field of vision, 103
focus
    balancing, 152
    directing, 221
forgetting play, 183
foundation skills checklist, 23–25
front cross
    about, 61–62
    common issues, 68–69
    direction changes and, 62
    handling sequences, 66–68
    high-tech, 63
    intermediate course example, 170–171
    mental practice, 69

    practice sequences, 157, 159–160, 163–164, 166
    prerequisite skills, 62–63
    putting principles into action, 65–66
    teaching, 63–65
    teaching with serpentine, 120
fun, keeping agility, 17–21

G

games. *See* play
Garrett, Susan
    DVDs by, 244
    on foundation skills, 23
    on reinforcement systems, 203
    on running outside a curve, 56
    2 x 2 method, 125
    website for, 4
getting started on courses
    about, 131
    common issues, 136
    handling start line challenges, 132–134
    mental practice, 137
    prerequisite skills, 132
    teaching tough angles, 134–136

H

handling skills. *See also* readiness tests
    asking for too much, 182–183
    balancing focus, 152
    changing speeds, 43–51
    discriminations, 107–113
    driving the line, 91–97
    false turns, 99–105
    front cross, 61–69
    getting started on courses, 131–137
    improving with video, 221
    isolating common mistakes, 222–223
    lateral distance, 35–41
    180-degree turns, 81–89
    preliminary considerations, 33

rear cross, 71–79
serpentines, 115–121
shoulder pull, 53–59
strategizing techniques, 142
270-degree turns, 81–89
using video to improve, 221–223
weave pole entries, 123–129
heel command, 23, 27, 191

I

identifying challenges, 143, 145–147
intermediate agility
    beginner versus, 11–14, 174
    transitioning to, 14–15
invisible dogs, 143

J

J & J Dog Supplies website, 245
jumps
    handling front cross, 66–68
    height considerations, 37, 84
    in a line, 39–40
    maximizing use, 232–233
    missing, 207
    purchasing, 232
    rear cross warnings, 77
    verbal commands and, 117
    warm-up, 231–233

K

The Kennel Club, 244

L

lateral distance
    common issues, 40
    mental practice, 41
    practice sequences, 164–165
    prerequisite skills, 35
    teaching jumps in a line, 39–40
    teaching pinwheel, 35–39

M

managing nerves, 225–229
Mayer, Diane Peters, 226, 228, 244
Mecklenberg, Linda, 194
memorizing courses, 215–219, 232
mistakes
    avoiding blame, 17, 21
    beginner versus intermediate levels, 13–14
    during false turns, 102
motivational issues
    de-motivating behaviors, 180–185
    learning to dance, 179–180
multi-skill practice sequences, 157–167

N

NADAC (North American Dog Agility
        Association)
    competition classes, 15
    contact information, 244
    record keeping and, 236
    on repositioning dogs, 202
negative reactions, 180–181
nerves, ring, 225–229
90-degree turn, 53–59
North American Dog Agility Association
        (NADAC)
    competition classes, 15
    contact information, 244
    record keeping and, 236
    on repositioning dogs, 202
novice level. See beginner agility
Nylabone, 183, 192, 209

O

obstacles. See also specific obstacles
    balancing focus, 152
    blocking, 132
    bridges for, 208
    checking body language, 59
    contact zones and, 27–28

The Intermediate's Guide to Dog Agility

on a curve, 25–26
diagram key, 240
getting started on courses, 131–137
handling, 68, 172
including in training, 167
looking at, 93
observing flow, 141
speed and, 28–29
walk-through considerations, 141–143,
   216–217
180-degree turns
   about, 81–82
   common issues, 88
   mental practice, 88–89
   practice sequences, 161–162
   prerequisite skills, 82
   sequences with wide turns, 88
   teaching, 82–85
openings, practice sequences for, 158, 161–163

P
performances, slow, 183–184, 226
play
   de-stick game, 192–193
   forgetting, 183
   reteaching the stay, 199–201
post turn, 53–59
practice sequences, multi-skill, 157–167
preparing for longer sequences
   backchaining, 149–153
   confidence and, 146
   identifying challenges, 143, 145–147
   intermediate courses, 169–175
   running invisible dogs, 143
   walk-throughs, 141–143
problem-solving
   effective techniques, 205–211
   mental practice, 209–210
   motivational issues, 179–185
   recapturing lost contacts, 187–195

reteaching the stay, 197–203
proofing process, 21
pushing strategy, 91–92

Q
quality, emphasizing, 19
quick releases, 189, 191

R
readiness tests
   agility skills checklist, 25–31
   foundation skills checklist, 23–25
rear cross
   about, 71–72
   common issues, 78
   handling sequence, 75–78
   mental practice, 78–79
   practice sequences, 157–158, 162, 165
   practice warnings, 77
   prerequisite skills, 72
   teaching, 72–75
recall command, 23
record keeping, 235–237, 241–243
refusals, 14
reinforcement systems, 203
releases, quick, 189, 191
repositioning dogs, 202
retraining
   natural part of process, 21
   stay command, 197–203
reward system
   cookie delivery, 19–20, 181
   delaying rewards, 184–185
   predictability of, 183
   reconsidering, 189–190
   warm-up jumps and, 233
ring nerves, 225–229
running contact, 194–195

The Intermediate's Guide to Dog Agility

Photo Credits

Peter Betts (Shutterstock): 10, 32–33, 148

Kelly Boyer: 192

Micky von Broen: 58, 60, 80, 87 (9.G, 9.H), 90, 95, 98

Andraž Cerar (Shutterstock): spine, 14, 154–155, 178, 182

Bob Denelzen (Shutterstock): 211

cynoclub (Shutterstock): 1

Dennis Donohue (Shutterstock): 30, 214, 224, 229, 234

John Evans (Shutterstock): 25

Margo Harrison (Shutterstock): 174, 230

Nick Hayes (Shutterstock): 52, 79, 92, 212–213

Mark Herreid (Shutterstock): 22, 228

Shawn Hine (Shutterstock): 196

George Lee (Shutterstock): 156, 245

Tracy Libby: front cover

Maureen Lyons: 34, 36, 38, 39, 41, 44, 46, 49, 50, 54, 55, 57, 64, 72, 74, 76, 82, 83, 87 (9.D–9.F), 101, 104, 108, 113, 118, 119, 122, 124, 128, 130, 133, 134, 137, 150, 190, 195, 199, 201, 202, 206, 209, 231, 233

Mackland (Shutterstock): 238, back cover

Ellen Perlson: 142

Petspicture (Shutterstock): 42

Shutterstock: 4–5, 13, 18, 28, 70, 111, 138–139, 158, 168, 180, 184, 186, 226

Graham Taylor (Shutterstock): 144

teekaygee (Shutterstock): 16, 69

Barb Triol: 106, 140, 188, 216, 220, 222

vgm (Shutterstock): 176–177

George Will (Shutterstock): 67

Zenotri (Shutterstock): 204

All other photos courtesy of TFH archives

The Intermediate's Guide to Dog Agility

Acknowledgments

My teacher, Lauri Plummer, continues to inspire me with her understanding of dogs and the sport of agility. Her insights are woven into these chapters.

Many thanks to Maureen and Jeff Lyons for the use of their agility facility to take photos. Thanks to Maureen Lyons for acting as lead photographer and to Micky Von Broen, Kelly Boyer, and Barb Triol for providing additional photographs.

I am grateful to my students and friends who modeled for the skills presented in each chapter. And to their patient dogs who ran exercise after exercise until we got the perfect shot, you are the best.

About the Author

Laurie Leach is an agility competitor on the local and national level. She teaches agility from beginning to advanced levels to students just like you. Known for keeping instruction both simple and fun, Laurie has built a devoted following of students and readers. Laurie's first book, *The Beginner's Guide to Dog Agility*, laid the groundwork for many students' agility careers. She has also competed in obedience trials and raced sled dogs. Laurie lives in Windsor, California.

NATURAL with added VITAMINS

Nutri Dent®

Promotes Optimal Dental Health!

Visit nylabone.com
Join Club NYLA!
get coupons &
product
information

360° Design
Cleaning Action!™

USA MADE

Dogs L♥ve 'em!

AVAILABLE IN MULTIPLE SIZES AND FLAVORS.

Nylabone®
Trusted for Over 50 Years

A275